THE POETRY TRIALS

TEEN SPIRIT

Edited by Lisa Adlam

First published in Great Britain in 2016 by:

 Young**Writers**

Remus House
Coltsfoot Drive
Peterborough
PE2 9BF
Telephone: 01733 890066
Website: www.youngwriters.co.uk

FOREWORD

Welcome, Reader!

For Young Writers' latest competition, *The Poetry Trials*, we gave secondary school students nationwide the challenge of writing a poem. They were given the option of choosing a restrictive poetic technique, or to choose any poetic style of their choice. They rose to the challenge magnificently, with young writers up and down the country displaying their poetic flair.

We chose poems for publication based on style, expression, imagination and technical skill. The result is this entertaining collection full of diverse and imaginative poetry, which is also a delightful keepsake to look back on in years to come.

Here at Young Writers our aim is to encourage creativity in the next generation and to inspire a love of the written word, so it's great to get such an amazing response, with some absolutely fantastic poems. It made choosing the winners extremely difficult, so well done to *Jessica Chan* who has been chosen as the best in this book. Their poem will go into a shortlist from which the top 5 poets will be selected to compete for the ultimate Poetry Trials prize.

I'd like to congratulate all the young poets in *The Poetry Trials – Teen Spirit* – I hope this inspires them to continue with their creative writing.

Jenni Bannister

Editorial Manager

A POEM IS JUST THE BEGINNING...

CONTENTS

THE POEMS

I HAVE FORGOTTEN AGAIN

The lacklustre melody of a flute, travelling through the winds,
awakes me with an involuntary jolt.
Echoes of pain travel up my leg,
Reaching the stump where an arm should be,
Skimming a hole where a heart should be.

I gulp from the flask, embossed with patterns of gold,
Hidden behind the trees, ale dripping down my shaking chin.
I sit silently.
I hear their protests, distinct in passion, unparalleled in pleading.
I hear their screams, the way they run, the way the silver of the
knight's sword cuts cleanly,
Through their helpless bodies.
Tears flow waywardly across the wrinkled surface of my face,
Guilt seeping from my dim pupils, so deeply embedded in their
sockets,
Knowing I did this.

And then I stop,
I have forgotten.
Again.

I hit my head,
To recall,
But I am greeted with an empty abyss,
Void of memories.
I scurry through my bag, brimming with stolen haberdashery,
A telescope emerges.
Telescope aimed high, squinting,
The tarnished sky sliced cleanly, a white smoke separation.
Airstrike.
Remnants of genocide, remnants of my family's death.
I sob and laugh, immeasurably deranged.

And then I stop.
I have forgotten again.

Faiza Manzoor (15)

FOREVER GROUNDED

There once was a girl
Named Jessica Light
She lived in New York
A city so bright
She thought she could fly
Way up in the sky
Now she's forever grounded

In the crowded streets
And busy school
She had no friends, she
Was a friendless mule
Used her, abused her
Broke her, accused her
Now she's forever grounded

She read lots of books
And watched all the shows
And from her lips
The words would flow
Her pen on paper
Like a smoking crater
Now she's forever grounded

As long as she read
They would never leave
They showed her new lands
And made her believe
'Stay with us forever
We can be together.'
Now she's forever grounded

'You know you can fly!'
The characters told
'You can join us here
No need to grow old!
Climb the Empire State
Accept your own fate.'
Now she's forever grounded

She climbed the long stairs
At last reached the top
She looked at the street
And finally stopped
Someone saw the girl
'Somebody stop her
She'll be forever grounded!'

'Just leave her to die,
she has lived her life!'
Her tormentors agreed
Words sharp as a knife
The characters cried
'Give up, end your life!'
Now she's forever grounded

The wind in her hair
From the roof she fell
For a while she flew
Then she saw their betrayal
She couldn't fly or soar
So of her no more
Now she's forever grounded

Head was in the clouds
She never came down
Until one sad day
Gravity took hold
She learnt the harsh truth
And pleaded for a truce
Now she's forever grounded

Never got married
No husband or life
Never with child
No 'Call the midwife!'
She hit the stone ground
And now peace she found
At last, forever grounded.

Adaora Elliott (14)

FREQUENTLY ASKED BUT NOT VERY FREQUENTLY ANSWERED QUESTIONS ABOUT THE FUTURE

Welcome to the future, I know you have questions.
Want to know how I know?
Well, I can read your mind.
Yes, that's right,
I can read your mind.
So as for those thoughts you have,
About not having children so I never exist.
Forget those,
Some things are just meant to happen.
Oh and please filter your thoughts.
Let's be serious,
I don't want to know about how you're embarrassed
About wetting the bed last night.

Is it nice here? Oh, seriously?
Your world is overflowing with things that are messed up.
Ever heard of 'dystopia'?
Did all the novels go in one ear,
And out the other?
Oh, clichés of your time
They're so monotonous.
Nowadays we say,
'Things go through your brain without proper processing.'
They say it's scientifically more accurate.
I say,
Who cares? Who cares about them?
They make my life hell.
Newsflash!
I'll probably be killed for saying that.
And in case you really still do not get it.
Yes, I can hear your confused thoughts,
Swimming round your innocent minds.
It's horrible here.

How long has it been like that? Who knows
Who cares really? It is as it is as it is really.

Oh I hear
Those thoughts, what are those... those...
'Weapons' you are thinking of?
Oh,
Those things you lot use to fight with.
Don't know about how to make them.
That information was erased
Generations ago.
So your questions,
It's boring seeing blank minds.
Come on why don't...
How was information about weapons erased?
Mind control, friends, mind control.
Yes, that's right, my sweet innocent little daisies
Suffocated in the folds of your total lack of understanding.
I am like the sun.
I bring the light of knowledge, as all your ancients would say.
Shakespeare, Euripides, Virgil, all that rubbish.
So, yes, mind control.
Now we've cleared up that, any more?
Oh dear, Mind Police are here!
Told you I'd be killed for saying that stuff.
Anyhow, nice meeting you.
Hope I've enlightened you.
Got to fly...

Rebecca Thorne (17)

THE SILENT VISITOR

He creeps through the shadow of the night,
Steals through the darkness, hidden from sight,
Covers the world in a glittering case,
Slowly, slowly, pace by pace.

He does not rush, nor hesitate, nor slow,
Shooting spears of ice with his frosty bow,
The world, under his care, will be lost,
Hidden under a layer of hard, white frost.

Olivia Hornakova

INSIDE MY HEAD

Sometimes people ask me what I am afraid of
Usually I think for a moment
But end up saying the same thing each time:
'I am afraid of the dark'.
And people assume I mean physical darkness.
The lack of light
The place where children's monsters hide in the night,
Lying in wait for the young ones
The place where that harmless branch outside your window
Transforms into a bony hand,
Tapping menacingly on the pane
But of course not
I mean the darkness in my mind.
The tendrils of corruption
That slither out from the deep, hidden parts of my mind.
The tips lick my ankles temptingly,
Coaxing me deeper into the shadows.
Each time I take a step deeper,
They grow stronger and stronger
Soon they are strong enough to lift themselves up
To whisper faintly in my ear
That I will never be truly loved.
That I'm a disgrace.
That I should disappear.
They suggest the tempting proposition
Of opening my veins.
As I listen to these whispers, I unknowingly inch deeper bit by bit,
Allowing the tendrils and their voice to grow stronger.
Soon they begin to engulf me,
No longer gently coaxing me closer
As they pull me deeper and deeper against my will.
And their once-faint whispers
Become ear-shattering screams.
The darkness in my mind
Is not easily escaped.

And every once in a while
It takes hold of me once again.
And just because I now know how to fight it
Does not mean
It isn't... terrifying.

Jade Nikoloff (14)

RAMADAN

Fasting in the month of Ramadan,
Especially in the family of Mr Khan,
Sweet Indian dishes craving your mind,
Like old cogs in a grey, dull machine having to grind,
Your directions are a time machine,
Each and every step you take is certainly seen,
Walking graciously through your own ways,
Passing over thirty days,

Spices being thrown in the panicking pan,
High speed spinnings of the frantic fan,
Golden brown crispy pakoras sizzling,
Minty ice cold drinks fizzing,
Stress and hunger engulfing your mind,
Slotting hard work which is definite to find,

Your stomach is imagined as churning train tracks,
Your stomach is imagined as burning fierce fires,
Your stomach is imagined as zooming Ford Fiestas,
Your stomach is imagined as ancient buildings,

A testament from Allah,
Fulfilling his needs,
Reading and praying in a mosque, room, basement or cellar
Is what makes a heart clean

Delicious dates,
Ten days remaining,
An elated face, with sorrow fading,
Good deeds, no needs
Ramadan, a path towards Allah.

Halima Khan Mazar (14)

THEY SAY

They say, 'Stay strong. It's going to be okay.'
Do I have to endure another day? Why won't the problem ever go away?

They say, 'Be the better person. Just forget about it.'
How could I do nothing and just sit? How will that help me, even one bit?

They say, 'They're just bullies. They can't hurt you.'
Do you really think that's true? What am I supposed to do?

They say, 'Report them. Then they'll stop.'
Could you find me a policeman or a cop? Or somebody that won't let this case drop?

They say, 'You're exaggerating. You must be lying.'
Can't you see me crying? Do you see my tears drying?

They say, 'Be quiet. You're such a cry-baby.'
Don't you see? Won't you realise how much this is really affecting me?

They say, 'There's no need to shout. It's not a reason to scream.'
Does it feel nice to be last on the team? Or be bullied, to the extreme?

They say, 'That's not bullying. Not at all.'
Don't you see them push me up against the wall? Or hear all the names that they call?

They say, 'You're not the only one. Many people are laughed at.'
Could you even imagine, being ridiculed like that? Have you ever been called 'ugly', 'unworthy', and 'fat'?

They say, 'High school will end soon. You won't see them again.'
Why must I wait until then? Don't you know that they've been tormenting me since I was ten?

They say, 'You must have done something. There's no fire without smoke.'
Does anybody fathom that I was never the one to provoke? How could you blame me, as if it's some sort of joke?

They say, 'Don't listen. Just ignore.'
How long must I continue living like this for? Don't you see that I can't handle any more?

They say, 'You can cope. It won't always be like this.'
Can't you see something amiss? Will anybody help me get out of this abyss?

Anisah Isbag

THIS POEM...

This poem, is as a demonstration
Of my skills in explanation
Through metaphoric correlation
So I'd appreciate an ovation
But I'll be a little patient

Also, I made this poem as an appearance
Of my ever humble perseverance
To keep a rhythmic coherence
And a consistent adherence
To try and give this poem brilliance

Thirdly, this poem is the outcome
Of what my writer's block has become
So I well and truly hope everyone
Can understand what I've done
So I hope it's enjoyed by someone

Lastly, this poem has a purpose
But I need you to look close
I'll give you one clue as you go
The lines can strike any pose
But as a poem and prose.

Abiye Amachree (13)

EQUALITY

Equality,
We all have something in common,
But we fail to know what it is.
If we work together we will become better as one,
Equality is what we need.
It's simple: some are black, some are white,
Half are female, half are male
People think we are different but we have
The same mind, the same fingernails
The same heart, the same organs
And the same beginning and end
Mandela said 'No one is born hating another person
Because of the colour of a skin or background or his religion.
People learn to hate,
And if they can learn to hate,
They can be taught to love,
For love comes more naturally,
To the human heart than its opposite.'

I say again black and white may be
Different, but we still have equality.
Africans and Asian may be
Different, but we still have equality.
Look in the mirror and ask yourself
Who would be your friend Love or Hate?

All things may seem impossible,
But when it is accomplished it is not
The world isn't all sunshine and rainbows
It's a very mean and nasty place
But when we have equality it will be a better place.

Ayodeji Ojeniran (13)

THE DRAMA LLAMA

I'm a llama,
I'm practising drama,
And here I am on the set.
I'm wearing a wig,
Which is far too big,
And I'm wondering how hot I will get!

I'm playing a lord,
And here is my sword
But I don't get to use it at all.
So what is the point,
Of aching joints,
Of carrying a stupid prop sword?

I'm now in a box,
Cos the wig was too hot,
So I asked to become a tree.
I don't think the part,
Of a rich lord at heart,
Is the acting part for me!

And if memory serves,
I suffer from nerves,
So the show might not happen at all!
Cos if I look up,
I will automatically shut up,
And I would probably stagger and fall!

I don't know what I'm going to do,
I might go back home to Southern Peru.
I might carry on with the play and the drama,
Or I might buy a field and become a farmer.

So there we go, a farmer llama,
I wonder what's next,

Well that's another drama!

Amy Cook

MONEY

What is money?
It's currency,
It's rich as honey.

But it can make people bitter,
Less money for hard hitters,
And for lazy managers,
Get paid higher?

It's unfair,
That some people don't have a thing to wear.
And look at us,
Making a big fuss.

About tax,
Not realising bad acts.

But can it bring joy,
Like a favourite toy?
Maybe so,
I know!

Send money to charity
It would be clarity
And to pay it's not tricky

Money won't buy happiness
But giving will,
And it's such a thrill.
If you're selfish you'll face loneliness,

But use it wisely,
Or it'll drive you crazy,
But if you use it nicely,
Then you'll be respected by everybody.

And also don't forget these words
It could help in a crossword.

Peyush Gurung (11)

LITTLE NIPPERS

I hear a loud crack of thunder
Rain gushes down my face
Everyone is waiting for that gun to go off
The wind sends leaves dancing in the salty air
Bang!
I run as fast as my legs can take me, but my feet sink heavy in the wet sand
Water starts to splash against my ankles, then my knees.
A wave cascades towards me and I dive under like a dolphin, sleek and slippery
Crackle, snap!
My neck stiffens. I can't breathe.
I emerge from the sea, soggy seaweed falling from my hair
My eyes open, just in time to see another wave heading straight for me.
I try to run, but I'm frozen still, my legs don't work.
'Look out. Get out of the water. Run!' Voices echo, are they in my head?
Crash!
I am pulled under by the wave, then large hands appear and drag me from the water onto the shore.
'Can you hear me? How many fingers am I holding up?'
My neck isn't working, I can't see who's talking and sharp pains run up and down my spine
Pain pinching at my neck like electric shocks.
'Call the ambulance! Someone call triple zero!' What is happening? Who is talking? Am I going crazy?
I hear the piercing wail of sirens.
My feet are suddenly lifted off the ground and then I'm lying down, trying to make shapes out of the dark storm clouds above, but I can't see properly.
My vision blurs. Blackness. I wake inside a small room, my heartbeat's in time with the beeping of machines.

Jayda Faith Whitehill (13)

HUMAN SIN

It happens once, twice, three and four,
Five, six, seven, eight, nine, ten and even more.
We don't know what we can do,
Because as it began it will end with you.

We are so confused and we can't explain,
What helped and supported us to gain what we gained?
We think and struggle our hands clutching our heads,
But we still wake up in the morning and do it all over again.

Unable to stop and control,
Wielding powers still unknown.
It's a tyrant, a tormentor, your biggest oppressor,
Your worst nightmare, your greatest pleasure.

But we feed and live on it,
Eating away at your own soul bit by bit.
And then on that day,
You'll wish that you'd knelt down and prayed.

But it's gone like a flame already blown out,
Because you are the fool without a doubt.
And you wish you had the power to let it go,
But it's already gone and taken your soul.

And now there's no one home,
And we can't help but feel so alone.
This is the price you have to pay when you play with fire,
Without a doubt you are the biggest liar.

And the lies you have told will make you gasp and choke,
And despite the fire's warmth, your blood runs cold.
But you still try in vain to amend with those you've condemned,
But now you are the enemy and they are no longer your friends.

So can we still say that we don't know what to do?
Because just as it began it will end with you.

Maryam Rashid (15)

ESPOSE HUMANITY

Oh, India, such a beauteous turf I had come across.
Albeit, I had stumbled upon a squalid shack,
wooden, woven, weak, wounded, writhen -
such splendid and bright garments – of all colours hung upon it.
A man, rather fragile, flailing with a cluster of kids, sewing,
he told me his story lest I leave him destitute -
we held hands as I had such inclination to comfort him
and I struggled to contain my tears of pity.

What barbarous nature,
the lakes ought to turn to gall, and I would thenceforth attempt to
help everyone.
No endorsement was set for them to see the city,
nor did they ever get to see the grand mint sea.
All they accomplished was the creation of a pile of clothes, ready for
departure
this was the norm for that culture.
I could no longer bear such cruelty, because I wanted harmony.
Here they would be gratified in bliss to stay alive!
To gain a placebo was the thought of satisfaction because
paracetamol can really cure cardiovascular diseases infiltrating India.
The barbaric one, have you no decency?
They would pursue their career as the labourers
for a single penny it is worth here!
There, oh euphoric India, it's the contrary.
His little chef hat, something he wore and found on the streets, in the
slums.
His nocturnal and diurnal long dress he begged for, he wore.

The cycle of slavery would continue and he would perish in the end.
Sew, give, eat, sleep, and be afflicted upon, until you are effete.
Ladies and gentlemen, what if that was you?
Espouse humanity to retain this sense of sanity -
because I cannot bear to witness, nor can others, such profanity.

Melissa Deniz Hussain (14)

NOW WE HAVE THE CHANCE

As we walk through these streets we seem to forget
The people who once walked on them and yet
We don't remember those who never had a choice
They're the ones who never had a voice.

It may seem it was long ago
Like we needn't mind but did you know
It still happens every day
While we eat, sleep, work and play.

Just because someone is different, they're still human too
Deep down we're all the same; him, her, me and you.
We shouldn't punish those who don't seem the same
And it's even worse when no one takes the blame.

Rwanda, Bosnia and the Holocaust too
These are just to name a few
And all because some people decide
That these innocent people must have their freedom denied.

This to me is just not fair
But some just don't seem to care
There are people facing persecution
And trust me, there is a solution.
It shouldn't matter about your religion, colour or creed
It's all about respect, that's what we need.

I understand it's easier said than done
But we can do something about this, one by one,
Because, you see, these things can't ever be undone.

I know that this is a dark, sad time
And I can't change anything with a rhyme
But next time you are walking down the street
Stop and think about those who will never get to meet
The beautiful world you have beneath your feet.

Sophie Rae Harris (14)

SOCIETY

I sit at school
With the lads I call my friends
They seem pretty cool
Never caused concern, never did offend

Then one day was different
As before I even knew
One of my closest friends turned and said
'Is your dad the same religion as you?'

To a proud Sikh like me
This question seems absurd
But I know why he asks; he sees
His head is covered

With a turban, like Bin Laden does
They know Osama's a Muslim so my dad must be too
Automatically they've lost all trust
But what the media presents *isn't* true

They cry, 'All Muslims are terrorists!'
And this scares me so
Because even though
My dad is not a Muslim we all still look alike
Our colour of skin, our culture isn't white

However long we've lived here
We'll never be the same
We're somehow less desirable
Simply because of our names

Sound different and unfamiliar to them
Yes, we can be lovely and yes, we can be friends
But when it comes down to it
Who looks more lovely and true?
The outsider or the one who looks like you?

Japneet Kaur Hayer (16)

DARK LIGHT

Sweltering heat emanates from the sultry sun rays,
Luring you in
And at first appearing to be a sense of comfort,
A sense of faith,
But in reality, light is bright with deceit.

Ever heard of the phrase 'trick of the light'?
That is just what it is – a façade.
Its beaming presence is ludicrous.
Light pollution. Ultraviolet radiation. Skin cancer.
These are all the effects of the ruthless light.

And so we should all despise the sublime light,
For sunlight attacks with heat
And heat suppresses the parched, rough deserts,
Divine light is the source of devastating droughts,
Scorching heat from light initiates bushfires and
Devours all,
And yet we worship it.

The Devil himself is surrounded by light,
And thus drowns in fierce flames,
Light is destructive.
Relentless.

Warm days are getting warmer... and warmer,
Caused by the sun's radiation
Blankets too thick are drawing closer... and closer
To destroy all that we have,
The light is mocking you; where is your hope now?

Like roses, warm days have an appealing exterior,
But possess thorns of perspiration, confinement
And suffocation.

Light is dark.

Nikhita Patel (17)

A STILLNESS IN THE LOUD

When you look at an ocean,
the first thing you notice
are the roaring waves in motion.
The tide is the roiling waves that dip majestically,
rolling white-fringed, and on, and on, and on.

The undulating ripples seem to thrash violently against the shore,
devouring up personal items like keys
to be gone, wiped out, forever more.
The ebb and flow of the water churns relentlessly.
It must tire soon.

But the surge does not retreat,
showing no pattern, no predictability.
And predominantly, no defeat.
It continues to perform its dance of death,
beckoning the weak to step forward, to be claimed.

The water emits a chilled sea air,
while attempting to enchant us with its beauty,
luring victims closer and closer as if by dare.
It rages like a caged animal,
begging to be set free.

All of a sudden, it falls silent.
And it is frightening-this silence,
as if we are all waiting for the world to become louder.
But just remember:
Underneath that loudness,
of the majestic waves collapsing on top of each other,
there is a stillness that exists.
There is life.
And I believe that is what writing is about.
It is about finding that stillness.

Jessica Chan (14)

JAW-BREAKER

Armoured and resistant,
My layers are consistent,
An incessant battle to fracture,
A dribble upon drool which is abrupt,
You are a prisoner for an outcome so electrifying.

But when you shatter my walls,
For when my layers break,
I pulsate a sensation so great!
Which catches the eyes,
Of hopeless urchins,
Who wish you could put it at stake!

Colours upon colours,
To which are detonated,
Vibrant and so fluorescent.
To which upon this day I leave my mark,
To which your dialect may be forsaken.

Prodigious flavours I renounce,
Exotic, tropical and saccharine.
Chew after chew,
Upon which your portal relishes,
I try to sustain your happiness.

But as my time is limited,
I soon get blurted out.
Stuck to the floor,
Too ignorant to my enemies,
I lay hopeless and in despair.
Now my inner goodness is no longer sustained,
I get trod upon by betrayers,
I lay asleep, awaiting my end,
For once I was so luscious and sweet!

Alan Paul Kakkassery (15)

BLACK

As dark as the night, the essence of fright,
The raw feeling you get when you close your eyes,

The whisper of words, the flight of birds,
The howl of a wolf in the glow of the moon,

A warrior's sin, as a battle begins,
A mere breeze of demise on a winter's day,

A ballet's grace, a desolate face,
As you wonder with no destination

A twisted game, that speaks your name,
The tear that falls when you're lost in the world

A looking glass, that's made of brass,
A shard of mirror that reveals the truth

A suburban town, you start to drown,
In that mad little world inside your mind,

The crux of death, that holds your breath,
As you struggle to find lost hope in your life,

A thunderous crash, a lighting slash,
As make-up smears across her eyes

The end of all things, a moth's broken wings,
As you fall through the cracks of a broken place,

A swan on the lake, a voice starts to break,
As you hold it all in, but the crying won't stop

The absence of life, a delicate knife,
That haunting child's screams turn to silence,

The piercing stars, a lonely boy's scars,
The fight for his life, as all fades to black.

Madi Noakes (15)

WORD GAMES

I can never quite find the words
to express the way I feel about you.
It seems I too often draw
a row of indecipherable tiles
emblazoned with letters which I cannot
fathom into words.

Perhaps I should invent something
and hope you do not notice;
after all, the agreed-upon dictionary
does not contain enough words
to adequately describe your effect on me.

There is no word
that can convey the agony
of those jagged letters snagging in my throat
as I try to speak them.
So yet another day slips irrevocably by
with these sharp, unspoken words
lingering between us.

I cannot spell out
in seven chipped scrabble tiles
how much my every heartbeat hurts
whenever you are close by.

Perhaps, if I had a million more tiles,
and the whole world was a Scrabble board,
I could decode these jumbled thoughts
into something meaningful.
But there are not enough letters;
or perhaps I'm just not very good
at this game.

Holly Hunkin (18)

THE RICHEST MAN

The richest man I've ever known
sleeps on the street outside my home
in an ancient sleeping bag encrusted with mould -
smelly, ugly and cold.

There are rips in his shirt and holes in his shoes
but he cares not as, at the top of his lungs, he bellows the blues.
You see, although he's a mess and although he's alone
there's not one thing he desires that he doesn't own.

The sky, a mask of shattered glass above,
illuminates the two possessions for which he has most love:
a notepad, full of words – unspoken -
and a pen, battered and bent and broken.

Beside him, his riches remain,
reminding him again and again
of the mission he must fulfil:
to free the world of ignorance and greed and evil.

Poor as he may be,
the rich man says he's free.
'It's the wealthy who are imprisoned,
living within the confines of their own reason.'

So he scribbles and scrawls (and signs
his name), filling endless lines
with rhymes, metaphors and similes,
attempting to cure the ignorant man of his disease.

He vows to continue to smother the pavements with chalk,
educating innocent passers-by as they walk
until one day, he says, all the fools will listen,
and be forever freed from the moneyed man's prison.

Oliwia Geisler (17)

LOST IN THE SHADOWS

We raise our fists in fear of tonight
We gained no strength today
We turn our eyes to skies of stars
And dream ourselves away

Can't clap our hands to drumming hearts
What we find hard to say
Can't stamp our feet to stand as one
When life is looking grey

When shadows creep into your head
And make themselves at home
You want to hide and cry and scream
But you suffer alone

Your worries fall on top of you
Your hope sinks like a stone
So close your eyes to take a breath
Turn back and now they've grown

But stop your crying just this once
Those tears aren't worth your eyes
Society will take its toll
But don't you learn their lies

Your friends are there to keep you safe
No matter how it tries
To weasel on into your heart
And watch it while it cries

It's time to let go of the dark
So say all your goodbyes
And open up your soul to light
You'll see the darkness dies.

Hattie Brown (16)

DON'T BLAME ME

It wasn't my fault
That my doll decided to fly out of the car,
And how could you blame me
When the thief broke into the cookie jar?

My mum shouldn't have been angry,
When I decorated the bottom of the wall.
You see, I would've drawn it higher,
But I'm just not that tall.

Dad had no right to yell,
When I put my blanket in with his best tanks.
Pink really looks good on him,
But I didn't get so much as a thanks.

And why am I always suspect,
When my sister loses her teddy bear?
You see he *likes* it in my room,
And I can't stop him once he's there.

It wasn't animal cruelty,
To give our dog a new place to live.
Our old washing machine box was suitable,
It was a very thoughtful gift to give.

You can blame the aliens,
Or the monsters under my bed.
But whatever happens,
Please keep this in your head.

I didn't stain my dress,
When Granny came around for tea.
The jelly just wobbled right off the plate,
So *don't blame me!*

Chloe Sephton

25

BAD APPLES

The good fruits gather around the new tree
The seed
They stare at the hanging poisonous sprout
The rope
The apples writhe but to no avail
Destined
The apples bruise around their soft edges
Dying
Why do they squirm so much? The good fruit shout
Laughing
They knew this was their fate! Why challenge it?
Lying
They knew this was their beginning since birth
Unfair
Yet the bad apples still grow, not knowing -
Unjust
- When the vines stop gripping around their core
Struggles
The slither of life dimming inside them
...Stop it!

The good fruit turned raw, their lies pierced their hearts
Why us?
The bad apples turned healthy. They were pure.
It's not -
The rotten crowd reeked of infected fruit.
The truth!
They walked away, their scent stalking them close
We're not -
The truth was hidden behind their cursed mind...
Bad apples.

Isa-Louise Moriah Clarke (15)

A BIRD

A bird flies alone through the crisp, cool air
A lonely soul without a care

With a dappled tail and an orange beak
It observes, quietly, the human week

Oh how it wonders about these strange creatures' lives
What has made them resort to guns and knives?

Why did they deviate from nature's aims?
Why did they choose to make such games?

Games of death, misery and sorrow
Cold buildings that yell, 'Borrow, borrow!'

A bird's simple life may be limited and without pleasures
But it has simple aims and simple treasures

The bird eats, drinks and loves like humans do
But it has no need to pollute and fill the sea with goo

So why are such birds called animals and beasts
When humans are praised geniuses and given celebratory feasts

What gives humans the right to shoot birds like this one
When if a bird bites a human its life is pronounced 'Done'!

A bird can produce children like any human can
A bird can create a home but without the frying pan

The life of a bird has value as well
They're not just an object that humans can sell

So next time a human sees a bird in the sky
They should give it their admiration as it passes by.

Mia Skevington (17)

THE DEMON INSIDE

Slowly the white moon rises high
In the dark and blackened sky

No colours of stars to be seen
like the sky has been wiped clean

The cold air freezing my breath
My body trembles with the fear of death

Standing in the shadows of evil
Always smelling the time of mediaeval

Loitering up the street is the red devil
Always peeking through ground level

His bony hand feels like the heat of fire
Scraping my flesh like mesh and wire

I turn around to see the whiteness of his eyes
But all I see is the cold, clear skies

Tense and full of rage
Like a new born Mage

My body intensifies with the power of heat
as my hair is no longer neat

My skinless hands are now lava red
Horns grow on top of my hairless head

Talons embed in my rubber skin
Prickling like a needle or pin

Finally I'm almost free
This is the demon inside of me.

Melissa Wright (15)

BLIND BEHOLDERS

Behind a curtain of well-veiled deception,
The bombs dropped are beyond comprehension,
Because it's not the flesh, nor the bone they asunder,
But passion's art, and its commanding thunder.

Though you will not notice the swipe,
When eye's treachery does pass the pipe.
Then our humanity will grow colder,
Henceforth art is to the blind beholder.

How men of the past will fear the future,
When our diminished freedoms become fewer.
And paranoia desires all be acquiesced,
Under the right regime of the West.

The masses will not see their suppression,
For that will be left to the ruler's discretion.
Systems of conveyance will sow division,
Their greatest tool, they call television.

So when the mighty do conspire,
Hold in mind the Reichstag Fire,
And how Winston Smith knelt to the other,
He died loving Big Brother.

To Bernard's end we too can relate,
With our surveillance, soma and directed hate,
For which reason I cannot help but worry,
How long before I'm just a cell in the social body?

That's why in the 21st century it pays to be reticent;
Because you are guilty until proven innocent.

Ethan Moore

CUPID'S ANALOG ALWAYS TICKS

She, who connects you, is a stranger as she is so,
At the witching hour of party lights up in one's mind.
And she, a stranger to you no more,
Exchanges grins and personalities, yet, blank,
You proceed to think of she,
More and more,
Until you and she are one;
No longer both,
Just one.
The analogue ticks,
On one knee,
Presenting only precious stones of the prosperous ones we all know,
That she loves more than the rest of her wardrobe, with its plentiful
hangers.
Then the moment lodges in your throat,
Separate no longer – bound by eternal mortality,
The 'I do's glisten after days of loyalty and passion,
The analogue ticks,
Until you impede her office of labour,
And call 'I do not'.
But the I dos cannot go back,
And one stares at her soulful pupils,
With only hefty burdens of future ahead to face,
Because she loves one no more,
She loves a-'nother',
- Met inside the same place of a witching hour party as one met she,
And one is not angry,
One is now alone.

Isaac James Thomas (12)

BREAKING POINT

These wars I wage are worthless,
Only destroying myself,
Every blow I try to land, comes back, mirthless,
I feared for my fragile soul.
And it brings me to my knees,
Begging and thinking, *Please*,
Why can't I leave this all behind?
Why can't I go back to when the world was so damn happy?
Why can't I skip through fields of *flowers*,
Singing songs before life got c****y?
It hit me full force,
And ran through its course,
It flushed me all blank and clean.
Took all the fight out of me,
Made me rethink, then,
I became obsessed...
Just the sight of a bite would make me feel queasy,
Stomach rocking and roiling as I became uneasy,
Not a touch for fear of becoming disgusting,
Scrubbed raw in the shower I got rid of all my trusting,
Locked myself away from society in the prison of my mind,
Falling into the warped rhythm of life unjust and so unkind,
When it skipped
And my life
Became disjointed, full of jagged edges,
And my raw sobbing would drown any hope of happiness I still
harboured,
Would I ever get back from the fall and being broken?

Anna I Wright (14)

SEA GLASS ON THE SHORE

Shards of bygone rainbows,
Scattered along the shore,
Tiny snippets of our hope,
Our joy, our tears and more.
They crunch beneath my wandering feet,
A sign of hope to come.
Tiny shreds of magic,
With which the whole beach seems to hum.
The morning light, it bounces,
From each crack, corner and side.
Staining the shore with its joy,
And causing fears to hide.
Each piece is strange and different,
And when I look I see,
Not I, but many others,
Who look right back at me.
They are from every walk of life,
But our lives are still entwined,
For each of us once walked a beach,
And this is what we find:
Shards of bygone rainbows,
Scattered along the shore,
Tiny snippets of our hope,
Our joy, our tears and more.
They crunched beneath their wandering feet,
A sign of hope to come.
These tiny vessels of our love,
With which the whole world hums.

Amy Hampton (14)

DEEP INSIDE MY HEAD

The frustration!
Metal discs clash in my head,
Sounds of doom and spirits surging in my bloodstream,
Everlasting drums,
Bursting its way through barriers,
And the brakes are let go!
Downhill speeding at 90 miles per hour,
Swinging my arms to the rhythm of the twists and turns of direction,
The momentum gets faster and faster and faster, until...
Crash!
A slow and steady pulse struggling to continue,
My breath on the verge of nothing,
Blurred vision focusing on the light,
Heavy weights bring me down to darkness,
Drowning in its depth.
I am lost in a maze of endless tunnels,
But only one will lead me back to life,
Then slowly,
Out of the choking fog,
A sun beams its rays upon me,
Warming deep inside me,
I rise to the surface,
Willing it to last for ever,
But,
It is inevitable that everything will replay,
Again,
And again,
And again.

Sydney Johnson (13)

I REALLY WANT TO BE A POET

I really want to be a poet,
Famous all around,
Despite that, there is some problems
That seem to keep me down.

Publicity isn't easy at all,
In fact, it's hard as hell!
Poetry is only words rearranged,
And *everyone* can do that well.

The future is a shining star,
Full of hopes and dreams...
But all I see in my future, is
Words and English degrees!

Such a stressful life to own;
Finding my muse and all.
Yet I still don't think I've found it,
Maybe I'm only a rhyming fool?

I've realised that my future's hard,
So I'll work and work and work!
After all, writing this poem is helping...
Even if it *is* full of quirks.

Now, I don't really want to be a poet,
Considering I can't see any pros.
However, reading poetry puts a smile on my face,
And I want to do the same for others...

Only with my own.

Selesha Palmer

MY DEPRESSION

Sometimes I have nightmares around the middle of the night.

I wake up with damp cheeks, and
I look around, wondering
what that was all about.
I feel silly and retire back to my sleep
and I'm angry at myself, since
it took me an hour and a half to fall asleep
and I woke up again three hours later.

I have nightmares in the day, too -
when I'm at school, surrounded by my friends.
I'm laughing one second at a crude joke, and
looking around the next; I can't help but think that
I don't like anyone standing here near me.
The joke isn't funny at all. But I have to laugh.

I don't want to be alone again.

And I want to feel like anyone else,
and that I'm just as happy.

The lies I make are the closest I get,
and for some reason, my nightmares hold me back.
I get angry at myself again. I'm standing
alone with damp cheeks, and I look around,
wondering what that was all about. I feel silly and think -
what am I crying about?
Isn't it odd that I'm crying when I'm so blessed?

Maybe I remember too much.

Nadia Yussuf

THE TRIP THAT CHANGED MY LIFE...

A trip that changed my life...

A cluster of schoolchildren,
Laughing, joking,
Visiting such a thought-provoking
Yet awful place.

Unknown to them,
Who begin to drink and eat,
Right under their feet,
Lay the dead.

And then an ominous silence descended upon the group,
As they grieved in silence for every regiment and troop.

While they fell silent,
They realised how violent,
The war would have been,
How determined to win.

The party began to assemble,
And as their upper lips began to tremble,
They stared at a cemetery blurred with tears,
A history from 100 years.

These pupils' worlds have changed,
They've experienced our soldiers' suffering and pain.
Their innocent minds craved the truth -
Why did they have to die so early in their youth?

Holly Cobb (13)

YOU FEAR ME

I feel nothing.
You hold my senses in the palm of your pale hand.
Crushed it, ground it to form the foundational cement for your
network of lies.
To my demise,
You rose on my shoulders, grew ten foot,
Well I am 20 feet tall.
Tall enough to pluck the stars from the blanket of night; thrown over
my bruised, brown body.
Prick.
Like a crimson river, my blood flows out of its veins,
Pooling around your knife.
Am I granted the luxury of screaming? Must I lay still?
As all I hold dear flows away from me.
Take, take, take. I will give you my revenge.
My fire will burn so brightly that it will melt away the shackles that
bind me to you;
You will *never* touch me again.
Mark my words,
Tattoo them into your skin
That you may feel the pain I have suffered.
Crush and grind all that you have stolen.
I am twenty feet tall, You are ever so small.
I float, fly like an angel,
Unbothered by your feeble cries.
I used to fear you.
You fear me.

Okechukwu Atuanya (15)

THE SWARM OF TROPICAL FISH

Under the crashing waves,
The most beautiful fish ever seen,
Lay in the sea, not hot or cold,
Just slightly in between.

Different types of fish,
Angel, sword and gold,
Each one is as good as the other,
As far as I am told!

The colours of the swarm,
Are delightful to say the least,
They travel through the stormy seas,
From the west side, to the east.

The yellows, reds and blues,
And all the different shades,
Some are vivid, some are striking,
And some, the colour fades.

Some have big, sharp teeth,
Some are quick and speedy,
Some are slow and fierce,
Some are small and needy.

So when you're at the beach,
Swimming in the sea,
Beware of the sea life around you,
Swim away and leave them be.

Abbey Long

THE PASTURES NEW

I gaze onto the vast land expanse,
Laden with lush, silky grass,
Rocked by the calm and gentle breeze,
The beautiful spectacle of nature enabling time to drift past.

The blades of grass are emerald sabres,
Adorned and glistening with fresh morning dew,
Waltzing and swaying to the flow of dawn's gale,
I adore the wonderful pastures new.

On these fields, I lie, prance or frolic,
All emotion converted into an involuntary coo,
Because the meadows are my retreat and place of comfort,
Emptying from my mind; hatred, grief and rue.

The sun's fingers tickle my forehead,
As I inhale the cool, countryside air,
Stumbling around in awe like a drunkard,
And strolling around as if not having a single care.

These fields are my refuge and my shelter,
The pastures my bed, the cool gusts my blankets,
A place of relaxation, even for my ancient physique,
The unwinding hands of nature feeling so intimate.

These fruitful lands are a place for all,
Animals, humans, bugs and bees too,
Yielding pleasing crops and plants in abundance,
I adore the wonderful pastures new.

David Dickson (13)

UNKNOWN AND UNREMEMBERED

This life is but a fickle thing,
One day we're skin, another bone,
You may climb the tallest mountain,
But in the end, you'll die alone.

You walk the Earth like you know all,
Going about much duties,
Never thinking about important things,
Only simple beauties.

The dust you scatter with your hand,
Does go far and wide,
But such is life so easily gone,
Like the evening tide.

You may be rich, more likely poor,
Some things you cannot count,
Like cheerful smiles and all life's blessings,
No limits do exist to limit their amount.

Life is governed by two handles,
That tick upon a clock,
There is no key to stop it,
And if there was – no lock.

The way life is,
Before you came, you were unknown,
And when you go,
You will be unremembered.

Rehana Byrne

DEPRESSION

Depression is no easy thing to deal with,
Always messing with your emotions, like a tinkering locksmith!
Your thought becomes tormented, not knowing what to do,
And all you need is to have someone to look up to.

Dealing with a loss, is not an easy task,
But just come out of your shell, take off that mask.
Look towards the future, with a smile on your face,
The love of your family, you need to embrace.

If you try to ignore it, it will linger with you,
It will never leave; you have to break through!
Think to yourself, all the things you can achieve,
Just let go of the sorrow and start to believe.

Look at yourself, and just think of the chances,
Of you actually being here, and all of your advances.
To give yourself up to sadness, is a dreadful thing,
One day you'll have something to care about, maybe an offspring.

Depression is like a black hole, consuming everything,
You can just look towards the light; happiness it can bring.
So don't worry if you start to feel down,
It's all going to be okay, just remember not to frown!

Look at the present as an opportunity,
Get social with friends, become a unity.
Happiness is not something to question,
Something is, however, that is depression.

Solomon Ambler-Danyluk (12)

#THATAWKWARDMOMENTWHEN

#thatawkwardmomentwhen
I have no idea what to say,
ever.
#thatawkwardmomentwhen
I extend the hand of friendship
and get it bitten off.
#thatawkwardmomentwhen
my best friend of eight years
decides she hates me.
#thatawkwardmomentwhen
I'd like to apologise and start over
but I'm scared of what she'll do.

#thatawkwardmomentwhen
you'd like to say you're sorry
that you've been a horrible friend
but you're too late.
#thatawkwardmomentwhen
you realise I've moved on
and found better friends
who really care about me.

#thatawkwardmomentwhen
despite all you did to me
and all the hurt you caused
I'm nice to you anyway.

Lorelei Stroud (16)

MISSING IN ACTION

Crowds waiting in the streets
Watching, waiting.
Where are those they love most?
All around you,
They surround you.
People,
The lucky ones,
Those that have their backs.
They embrace
And the knot in your stomach gets tighter,
As you remember,
You will never see your man again.
For he is lost inbetween unmarked graves,
But will forever be in Flanders Fields.

Across the road your friend
Cries tears of joy,
As she spots her fiancé,
A couple of metres away.
You turn around suddenly,
As you feel a hand on your shoulder,
Hoping it would be Him.
No one there...
Just the cold shadow of a part of your heart
That is, 'Missing In Action'.

Rosa-May Bown

THE FUTURE

Wondering how the future will be, following this path of anxiety,
Discrimination and cruelty,
Is this all the world can offer to me?

Refugee and immigrant families;
Torn apart,
Slicing up the seams,
Shattering the heart.

The homeless,
Longing for a bed,
Wandering the streets,
Hoping to be fed.

The poorest parts of the world;
Far from civilisation,
Overflowing with poverty,
No food for their nation.

The sick around the world;
Countries with spreading disease,
Whether coughing, dying,
Or an uncontrollable sneeze.

Wondering how the future will be, following this path of anxiety,
Discrimination and cruelty,
Is this all the world can offer to me?

Ogorchukwu Ozor

WAR, FAMILY AND I

Before you take a shot
A baby sleeping soundly in a cot
But then there's a big sound
Kids flying around
This is cruel to humanity
The name for that is insanity
Just to clarify
There isn't time for hello or goodbye
People blown to bits
The family that splits
I've had enough of this
When you hear that hiss
You better run for it
But then you fall in a pit
Feeling sick
You don't know where your family is
You start looking around
You can't see them!
Your heart begins to pound
You start calling their name
No answer!
So you sit down in shame
Just wondering...
Why they wouldn't answer their name.

Farah Kossari (13)

FROZEN FURY

The howling of an angry bear,
The cold that burns my heart
And whips the wind above me.

Frozen tears that hammer
To the frosty ground below,
Tears of fury, anger, pique.

Buildings are now barren white
Blank canvases, ready to
Tell a story of Nature's beauty.

Trapped and scared behind
The closed doors of many houses,
No room for opportunity.

Shiver do the souls of
The old and young
In the heart of the frozen fury.

Till the storm passes,
And hope arrives as
People assess the damage done.

Once again they are safe
But not for long,
As they anger her once more.

Kirsty Richens (14)

YOU LOVE HIM, DON'T YOU?

You love him, don't you?
Not a name nor a face,
And someone came into place.
Glistening eyes,
Hoping not to hear goodbyes,
Just when everything went well,
You're the only one who stumbled and fell.

Chase your dreams
They said,
But are they the ones
Crying in bed?
Played you like machines
Bored after he used the first coin
In his pocket jeans.

Tears in your eyes?
'No,' I laughed as I lied.
They say mascara is expensive,
But my pain is priceless.

When will there be a time,
Where I can call you mine?
I'll wait by the bay,
For forever and a day.

Alfreda Rus (15)

SURGE OF THE CHARGED DISTURBANCE

An oppressed world of its own,
spiralled in waged war.
Soft, sweet clouds turn sickly,
Hardened like stones.

Blanched with anguish seeping across the sky;
blotched by the flare of swift pitch black darkness,
Devouring the heavens.
Pandemonium spits a brisk flash of a ghostly army.
You own everything that is nothing.

Slick silver sparks drive enraged,
through the breeze of the whipped wind
paralysing the sea – tight -
like a boa constrictor seizing its prey.

Rendered, disenfranchised, skidding,
Luminous silk is offered for mercy from frenzied fury.
The hunger of the thunder's rumbling
instils salted violence, which spills,
chills that drill,
Beyond the surface.

Jasmine Sekou (14)

THE RED SMOKE

When I get annoyed or angry at something or someone I can feel that
the red smoke is coming.
Only I can see the smoke.
It changes colour, from light grey to fiery red.
When the smoke comes, it forms a shadow on the outside of my body.
The flames burn every inch of my body.
No one else can see the burns.
No one can see my unbearable pain.
Only I can see the smoke.
I created the red smoke.

Sarah Louise Williams (17)

THE BOY WHO CRIED WOLF

Hiss.
Wind blew through the ruffles of the infamous liar's hair,
A cry for help echoed throughout the tall creatures,
Suspicion spread like a plague from one to another,
As the beast lurked in front of the pale boy,
The hawk had detected its prey.

Suddenly shivers had crawled up his fair skin,
Sweat formed in his clenched hands as his breathing accelerated
For an instant, he and its eyes connected before it shifted to its food.
Absent-mindedly the boy was howling, screeching,
The animal had vaulted over and into the enclosed pen,
Its fearsome teeth were revealed in almost a devilish smile,
As its bloodshot eyes danced to the chilling wind.

A cluster of the red-faced appeared with sunset flames on vicious stakes,
Horrified glances at the colourless boy who quivered amidst the wind,
A hoax wolf ceased to exist upon his own mind,
Now seen as the infamous deceiver,
Regret filled his brain as the past repeated itself,
Once more would he face the guilt, once more.

Sophie Singer (13)

LIFE

Life is an opportunity, make use of it
Life is a challenge, conquer it
Life is beauty, admire it
Life is a duty, complete it
Life is a game, play it
Life is a promise, fulfil it
Life is a tragedy, confront it
Life is an adventure, explore it
Life is precious, don't lose it
Life is life, fight for it.

Muhammad Amaan Kamar

THE GAMES IN MY ROOM

The video games that
I keep in my room,
like Tetris, Terraria,
Minecraft, and Doom,
and one about somebody
raiding a tomb,
and one with invaders from space...

They're up on the dresser
and down on the floor.
The Legend of Zelda
and Street Fighter IV,
Splatoon and Nintendo
Ms. Pac Man and more,
are scattered all over the place.

There's Sonic the Hedgehog
and Dragon Ball Z,
and Mario's Party,
and Madden for Wii,
and FIFA 15 for the
PlayStation 3.
They're littered and strewn all around.

Karim Eric Bennett (13)

THE WORLD'S END

We pack our bags and get ready to leave
The world is about to end, we need to flee
Earth now polluted, just rubble and bones
All people cared about were the latest phones
Here we are now, about to evacuate our world
We'll try to do better next year.
As we land up on the moon
We see our home gone much too soon.
People stare, upset and ashamed
As they pray we won't repeat the same.

Kacy-Marie Sutton (12)

TIGRESS

Her orange coat bleeds white and black,
she prowls around with claws out slack,
her murky eyes like pools in swamps,
every step she takes she stomps.

A face of probity is her façade,
But get too close and you'll be scarred,
Between the lips red – rich with blood,
She will make a crimson flood.

Her thirsty tongue that will devour,
She swipes as swiftly as a flower,
Her graceful leg and grasping paw,
One on one – a race to draw.

She knows she's faster than any man,
You'll end up dead without a plan,
Watch her delicate coat of fire,
Dancing in the grass of wire.

Camouflage barrel in the brush,
Booted footsteps quiet – hush,
Shot of power and hysteric cries,
All goes silent – fire dies.

Benjamin Jacob Garwood (15)

WHICH WAY OUT

Most things in life come with a cost, during this process many are lost
Risking their lives to benefit the greater good, anyone would save
them if they ever could
The doors were slowly closing, we're already too late
No longer could we survive, only my death awaits
However we're like no other, we survived
For that I got nominated, to join the runner's crew
Every 6am the runners would run, in search for hope,
if there ever was
Eventually we found a way, a way to end this all.

Monique Kaur Badwal (16)

SELFISH TO THE CORE

Why let them plead
If we have far more than we need?
Why let them continue to bleed:
If to them we have paid heed?

If the citizens need food
You can't just say you're not in the mood.
If a young citizen needs shelter
You can't just give it away to an elder!

If you knew someone was feeling low
What care would you show?
If you knew someone wasn't cared for
Would you care for them anymore?

If someone told you they were alone
Would you invite them to your home?
The answer to all the questions above
Is no!

Selfish human beings;
Selfish to the core;
Selfish human beings;
Always want more!

Chelsi Bouher-Theakston

WHAT THEY DO BEHIND CLOSED DOORS!

Boom! Crash! Bang!
There go the pans
This is to tell you
That Godzilla's around

You have to be quiet
You have to be mute
Or you won't get any soup

They beat you hard
Their screams will make you faint
And you sometimes don't have dinner
On your plate

What happens behind closed doors
Is what you can't see
Let hope the children are set free

This makes me scream
This makes me shout
Sometimes I don't know
What I am angry about.

Sharon Johnson (12)

I GO INTO BATTLE

I go into battle
I go into battle
With my armour of steel
Impenetrable and strong
My body's last defence
I go into the battle
With my breastplate of valour
Courageous and brave
I will never cower
I go into battle
On my steed of speed
Swift and sharp
I ride as fast as light
I go into battle
With my shield of protection
Unbreakable and serviceable
May my shield be my strength
I go into the battle
With my sword of power
May my enemies fall at my hand
As I win this battle.

Nimofe Wilson-Adu (13)

WE WILL REMEMBER THEM

The last words from officers they say;
'Go on! Go on!' as down came the rain of artillery bombs.
Now 100 years on from that horrific war,
We remember those men so, so poor!
The poppies among the graves, red as blood,
Which in the battles covered the mud.
War is futile, pointless and sad,
People who start them must be mad.
All the wars from then to today,
Those who died can safely say:
'For your tomorrow we gave our today.'

Matthew Williams (12)

ARE TEENS JUST MISUNDERSTOOD?

Although we cry, pry and sometimes get high!
Although we groan, moan and spend time on our phones!
It does not mean we're hormonal, we're just misunderstood

Although we hate, date and most of the time we procrastinate!
Although we break the rules, curfews and sometimes act like fools!
It does not mean we're hormonal, we're just so misunderstood

Although we complain, sound very vain and sometimes feel drained!
Although we mess up things, act like kings and play on heartstrings
It does not mean we're hormonal, we're just so very misunderstood

Although we know what's right but still cause fights and sneak
out at night!
Although we follow trends, spend time with friends and have no plan
to make a means to an end!
It does not mean we're hormonal, we're just so very deeply
misunderstood?

... I think?

Opeyemioluwa Adeleke

ART OF THE UNSEEN

Gliding my hand across the page,
I feel its rough texture,
I feel the slight wetness of the drying colours underneath my
fingertips,
But I am unable to see them,
I am unable to view the beauty of art that is right before my eyes.

People around me are cheering me on,
Praising my work hanging on the wall,
Whether it's in a museum, or my very own home,
I don't know,
All that matters at this very moment is
I have people by my side supporting what I love and live for.

Aleksandra Kaszewczuk (16)

THE BREAKING WAR

Pitch-black night.
The moon shines upon the sleeping city.
The dusty buildings stop smoking.
All is quiet.
Suddenly, sirens blare.
The city woke with a sudden boost of alacrity.
Children hid under beds.
Guns gazed into the sky.
Plane engines warmed up.
Then it all began.
Bullets whirled through the sky,
But faced nothing more than repelling off the metal tin falling to the ground.
The lucky ones manage to sink into human beds causing little effect.
Then the gate opens.
A huge piece of steaming metal began bouncing.
Before a feral finger pushed a button to send it down.
Then it begins.
To fall.
To drop.
Withstanding billions of bullets.
Before it lands with a,
Bang!

Abdullah Mahdi Syed (12)

LONDON OF MY LIFE

I used to live in London, it was a perfect life,
Until I moved to Bradford and made a new start overnight,
Now my story has taken a twist in time,
For now I live here with a mark of treachery behind.

My past would show London was different but brilliant,
I used to have fancy balls and galas every Friday midnight,
But here people do everything to their fulfilment,
I wish I could go back because sometimes my life was like a
delicious delight.

When the mark of treachery had fallen behind,
That's when I began to fall... My friends began to show me the light
and helped me,
I may not know what the future holds... day or night,
I'll show there is another side to me you can't deny,

Popularity is all that I desired,
Like a phoenix burning bright in the sky...
But hear when I say, that my past does not define me, that I will not
be required
'Cause my past is not today.

Narjis Fatima Rizvi (13)

YOU

I'll remember the glassy reflection of my face in your eyes
every time our bodies were inches apart.
And the way they mesmerised me even though they held no
emotions on your behalf.
Your touch so playful, yet so guarded,
confused me.
And you left me alone; dazed about how you could feign such desire.

And so I'll steal the air from your lungs,
leaving you gasping for peace.
And I'll burn my face into your mind
So every thought of me leaves you sorry.
But most of all, I'll wreck every memory you ever held sacred
So you're more broken than the shattered pieces of my heart
as you left me wondering why you ever held my hand so delicately.

And as nostalgia kicks in,
the only thing you'll feel is the burning of your throat as you try to
forget the taste of my
Love.

Mahnoor Siddiqui (16)

THE LAND OF TOMORROW

The Land of Tomorrow is different to today
You will see it in a very different way
Today you have an apple, tomorrow you may not
Things will be different, a little or a lot
No one knows, except for those
Who believe that they can change it
Whether it is bad or good
Or is meant to be misunderstood
Whatever it is just let it be
A lot of people cannot see
What is on the other side
The side that no one really knows
Except those who create it.

Alex Hamilton

EMPTY REASONS

I sat and watched and wondered, life until they blink
Millions and trillions, eternity till sleep
Bright lamps burning till the bleeding taste of death
Starlight turns to dust, bright light at its last breath
An even further stretch of never-ending sky
Life so far a fetch and empty reasons why
A puny little galaxy, barely learnt to stand
Holds a tiny Milky Way and home to mighty Man
Upon a helpless planet, just a dot amongst it all
That doesn't even shine, so miniscule, so small
I invite you to think how unimportant each of you may be
To the sky that stretches further than insanity can see
So pillage, rape and murder, damage as you please
This tiny dot, not even a spot, of a world ridden in disease
But know the dust within your touch once lay amongst the stars
And will again someday, coming when our dot has gone too far
Nothing will be left but perhaps your dust might shine
A little brighter than the rest if you decide to skip the why.

Imogen Quadling

IMAGINE

Imagine what it would be like to be a bird,
To be in a herd or Henry the Third,
Swishing and swirling; flying in the breeze,
Above the park where children break their knees.
Big food, hampers and a golden crown,
King of the castle, on top of the mound.
Imagine what it would be like to be a shark,
A shark that is beached on top of a park,
Swinging on swings, and sliding down slides,
Waiting for the moment when the evening tides rise.
Imagine what it would be like to be a crab,
To work as an agent, or in a bio-chemistry lab,
Mixing the chemicals, think of the money you'll have.
All of this for his beloved American lady crab.

Dylan Wenman (11)

LOVE CONQUERS ALL

A wrecked ship explores the sea of my pain,
Tears gush down like waterfalls and rain.

You only weaved webs of deceptive lies,
Your betrayal painted itself across the night skies.

If only we were relentless and passionately burning like coal,
But we only had a flame that was ignorant and naive like your
flickering soul.

The world was a canvas for us to paint,
But because of you my imagination was under restraint,

I now realise I committed to the wrong path,
You corrupted me with anger and a devilish wrath.

Now my eyes are windows to a hidden world of despair,
Only because you were too cruel to care.

Didn't you realise love conquers all?
For now this soul can reach the heavens and never again fall.

Amiera Sharif

THE NIGHT'S ALIVE!

The night is dark,
Its silence is deep,
Now the sun has gone to sleep.
So, while the wind howls,
And the clouds cry,
Twinkling stars dance to the tunes of the night sky!

In the dark, far away,
a shooting star coming this way.
It passes the moon, the mascot of the sky,
Its light so bright
It blinds my eyes.
And in a flash we say our goodbyes!

Noor Khan (11)

NEVER LOOK UP...

Outside the window people are fighting
It does not look at all inviting
But we wouldn't know would we?
We never really look up

Wow, look at the stars!
Shining down on those beautiful cars
But we wouldn't see it would we?
We never really look up

There's your future lover
Who you might never actually discover,
You never looked up

Lots of things happen
That we never notice as we are trapped
Trapped by the technology around us
But we wouldn't notice would we?
We never really look up.

Esther Gbadebo (12)

THE RISE OF ISIS

Corruption, deception and hate.
Over them the world has come to a debate
About whether they, ISIS, are the real Islam,
The true Islam. The one where the definition is peace.

But know that ISIS and Islam has never
And will never be one religion.
Because Islam is peace and not slaughter,
Where you kill your own daughter.
And leave your son.

What's done is done,
We can't change that.
But know ISIS, you will be overcome,
Your dictatorship a pile of ashes
And your cruelty, your doom.

Mariam Bibi

THE INVISIBLE ILLNESS

The feeling you get when you have nowhere to go
Those emotions that build up and are hard to show
And the thoughts that flow through your head
Make you wish that you had never fled.

But then you think to yourself who would have known
About those hurtful emotions that had quickly grown
And how horrible you were feeling back there
And to stay, you know you wouldn't have dared

You think of your family and how they must feel
Then the memories come back so fresh and real
You need some time to clear your head
But to admit to your depression is your biggest dread

I know I need help to get through this phase
Even if it takes one thousand days
I ran away to gain time to confess
To all that I love, that I am depressed.

Ellie Lily Elsie Rose Victoria Fennell (16)

WORDS

Words, aren't they funny?
Through actions wars are started, through words wars are ended.
Words can be so many things, ones of love, hope and passion
Ones of hatred and despair

Words are what make us human
Everybody knows some form of language, and in that language words
We have evolved to be able to do so many things, yet without words
nothing would be known.
Through words people can live for thousands of years

Go down through the ages, becoming a legend.
Through words people live forever, or they die in the dust.
So many untold stories as people have forgotten the words
Words are powerful things.
Words of love and hope, or hatred and despair.

Ailie Mira Ruth Keddie (15)

FAILED

My life was ruined, destroyed by war,
Never knew what I gave my old life for,
Never had hope, never was free,
A life of anguish – all it could be.

Was overcast and drowned in sin,
No good blood left, nothing within,
Dark thoughts struck, was dazed with fear,
Knew the end wouldn't come, never was near.

Torture never left, wouldn't let me die,
For everything I did, my soul would cry,
Was filled with sin, all my blood drained out,
Left there hopeless, riddled with doubt.

New death awaited, came with every new day,
Pain never left, couldn't wash it away,
Charred in black blood, wouldn't let me flee,
Sinned all over, I failed me.

Elliott Denning

WE ARE HUMAN

Sometimes, we are shut out from reality
Sometimes, we are in the middle of it
Sometimes, even, we dance as puppets of fear.

We are toys, flowers, and thorns
We are learning new things, for better or for worse
We, even, dance as puppets of fear.

Do we know tomorrow?
The dawn of a new day, a new life?
Do we, dance as puppets, entertaining ourselves?

We change, we morph
We are different, not toys with strings, not an everlasting hero
But don't we get to see the dawn of a new day as we are?

And we are human.

Lauren Wong (12)

A SIP OF SUMMER

The searing sun is out,
Rich fields with tulips all about,
The delicate birds are tweeting away,
And relishing the summer's day,
Everyone puts their sunglasses on,
Ready to watch the marathon!

It's my favourite time of year,
When the neon sky is clear,
The perfect time to bathe on the beach,
No teachers are here to teach,
People are reading their magazine,
Whilst others cover their mouth in ice cream!

Summer is going but will come again soon,
Close your eyes and wish for next June,
Back to school children will go,
And slowly see brown autumn leaves blow!

Nabilah Rahman (14)

BULLYING

Bullying is a pernicious crime,
It's something that happens for a long time,
You may want to run away,
And treat it like a normal day,
But tomorrow it'll happen again.
The same old pain
Will haunt your brain,
There's nowhere to disappear,
From all this rage and fear.
Tell somebody that you're on the run,
And hopefully the bullies will be done,
Freedom will be yours,
You won't be scared to go outdoors,
Because you're stress-free at last,
Never to be intimidated or harassed!

Zakiya Rahman (12)

LIFE

An everlasting potion
Sprinkled with emotion
Topped off with the government's proclamation
But what is the point of our reincarnation
Life is conduction
So there is always an assumption
From one place to another
Life jumps over hurdles
With clear communication and connection
Life never fails
It has no logic
So it doesn't feel affection
Life has no condition
So it is always energy efficient
Life is...
Precious.

Amman Ahmed

THE CONSCIENCE

The conscience inside my head talks to me,
Telling me to do things that shouldn't be.
Red and blue flashes, with a siren and all
Racing towards me like I'm a criminal.
Conscience, conscience, oh what did you do?
Telling me to do things I shouldn't do.

'Hands up!' one man shouts at me,
'Or you'll be coming to the cell with me.'
My conscience resists, I couldn't do this
Spending my life without my sis.
Running away my conscience says
'Don't resist, you won't be missed.'

Muffled shouts, overlapped by the thudding of my heart.
'Come back!' I hear one say, 'Or you won't see light today.'
Bang, bang, bang!

Katelyn Roache (12)

WHY THE CROW WEARS BLACK

The crow flies high,
Above a ruined field,
The earth now red,
Where kings have kneeled.
The crow flies low,
Through the dead trunks of trees,
At their roots, greatcoats strewn,
Riddled with fleas.
The crow pecks and scrapes,
At the body of a knight,
Lain beside others,
Who share the same blight.
The crow deals in death,
More than any of its kind,
Damnable work,
But he does it with pride.
You see now child,
Why the crow wears black,
For it is his burden alone,
To carry the damned souls back.

Jordan Rollinson (15)

SORROW

Gawking at the luminous moon
Trapped in a forest of remorse and horror
From the world I once knew
Stuck in a hole of torture
Remembering the past of horror
When I was discriminated
I was a stain on a white blanket
A crack on a titanium plate
A galaxy of pain was endowed me
I felt like a shadow in the jet black night
Wanting to run, jump, fly from the evil of the world
Inside the innocence of my head raged a storm
Showing anger, frustration and animosity
My anger a captive animal not shown to the arrogant earth
My pain an exasperated volcano not erupted
Inside me lay a bomb which could explode at any time
To me hope's a myth, love a legend and pain a promise
A tear ran down a cheek as I stared out of my bedroom window at
the evil of man
My human rights turned to dust in a desert of snakes
My emotions turned torn apart like a delicate paper
Was change possible? What lay ahead after this life?
As the bright light faded away a bead ran down my cheek.

Zeeshan Raja (13)
Al Khair Secondary School, Croydon

THE WOODS RE-BIRTH

'Do not pity them
Their tears
For they still have the
Strength to weep.
Pity the soulless
The frozen ones
Who have forgotten
What it is like to cry' – Nathan Griffith

The woods re-birth
Nyx's black cloak surrounds me, neon stars of blue and grey
scattered upon her lazy brow.
Winter's cold breeze caresses my bare nape, willows sway to the
wind's sour melody.
Artemis' silver chariot hovers, pulled by a golden horned deer.
Apollo's brow creases, yet to be re-born

Stretches of rose and elder flower lay suspended in time under a
sheet of cobalt frost
Brambles block my path, thorns beckoning me towards them as I look
longingly to the other side; where the sun shines and the birds chirp
O how I wish I could join the other side!

I strain my ears and I hear the faint trickle of a stream, the water
gurgling happily
I sniff the air and smell the faint but delicious aroma of summer.
Alas I am stuck in this frozen wasteland
Alas I await the re-birth of the woods!
When the flowers will start to bloom and the animals will wake up
from their deep sleep.
The birds will chirrup once again,
A synthesised melody created as Pan plays his sweet flute.
O how I wish I could join the other side!

Pierced by a thorn, I try to remove it with a trembling hand
I howl as it pierces through my soft flesh.
My blood falls slowly turning the frozen sapphire ground a deep
shade of crimson red.
My whole body burns with passion and anger,
Blood flows from every pore.

I fall to my knees, the pain is unbearable, the silence rings loud
in my ears.
It all goes black, it is so pure and so dark it is mesmerising to look at.
It's all over, all gone, I am greeting death.
Yet, the black starts to fade, and with the declining darkness, new
knowledge comes.

I begin to realise that I have been here all along
O finally! Shades of greens, browns and yellows merge, forming the
paradise I had yearned for so deeply.
Hues of mystical colours. I look around eyes wide, I strain my
ears eagerly.
The birds are chirping, the stream is gurgling.
The sun warms my bare nape, I sit up, ardent with joy, oh I am
finally here!
There was never another side. My eyes have finally opened, I have
left the cave
The shadows revealing themselves to be pieces of abstract beauty
My chains of ignorance and stubbornness no longer holding me down
Trapped and deluded but now a bird set free
A mental cage unlocked

RIP Plato

Adam Izeboudjene (14)
Al Khair Secondary School, Croydon

BEYOND THE WINDOW, BEYOND MY EYE

As I sit behind the window,
I look upon the world,
But ne'er inside have I had a feeling so curl'd,
I feel as though I'm trapped and my heart has turned to dough,
My view is always fallible as I tune onto the crow,
I look upon the blossoms, their surfaces pearl'd,
Forever dreaming of a heart that is unfurl'd
A heart is ready to be moulded, this heart is... Oh!

Years after years have dragged me by,
Finally the window is open,
As I put my head through and feel the breeze I start to cry,
Now I can put my head through and turn to the raven,
Finally I can see the whole of the picture, with the whole of my eye,
Now I can see the world, twisted and misshapen.

Abdullah Nabeel Ul-Haq (14)
Al Khair Secondary School, Croydon

A WISH

Where there was a knife,
Of course, there was no life.
Where there was a pipe,
There wasn't any life.
You were shouting, 'Papi!'
But it was too late to stop it.
I was doing sins, right,
And you were doing nothing.

I wish I was alive.
I wish I could do it.
You seemed to be an honest person,
That's all I wished from my heart.
- But I'm stupid, I was wrong.

Arman Madani
Alexanders College, Woodbridge

THANK YOU

Roses are red,
I have a phone,
Nobody texts me,
Plane mode – on.

I don't want to hear
Anything from you,
You were not here
When I needed you.

Won't deny, I miss time
Spent next to you,
It seemed to me a crime
To ignore you, it's true.

But everything is changing,
And people changing too,
I become more demanding,
Now I know what to do.

You made me independent,
This feature is brand-new,
Now I don't trust people,
Thank you.

But I don't want it to be
One more depressing story,
There are still people in the world
Whose hearts are full of glory.

Valeriia Dumenko (15)
Alexanders College, Woodbridge

SUCCESSFUL REQUIEM

I love you,
I gave all my heart to you when I first heard of it.
Heard of A Little Night Music while an orchestra was playing out
loud in a banquet.
You made that little night into a wonderful night and the best
night ever!

Everyone would fall in love with you, if you were still here.
I can hear A Little Night, Symphony and Concerto that you invented,
every day, every time and every night.
Before I go to school, while I rest and while I dream of you at night.

Symphony.
Your symphony takes me back to 1788 when it was performed by
you, with your cheerfulness, mightiness and your anger.
I can feel it all through the symphony.
No one can hear you but I do! Show them! Prove to them that you
are the best!
Please play it out loud! It will be there forever! No one can pull
it down.
Louder, louder, you can make it more and more
As loud as you want them to hear, people from all around the world
would hear it,
Hear that cheerfulness, mightiness, anger, anything that they should,
because it is amazing.

But you are not here anymore, sadness has dominated and requiem
has begun.
I want to shout out very loud, as loud as I can, until I have no
voice left.
Or is this time for you to rest, sleep well.
Every day I say your name out to remind people that once upon a
time you were alive,
You were working hard, very hard to handle. Please rest.
You have made everyone smile, that's enough. Please rest. I would
regret it.
When illness comes, you cannot stop it. An evil that no one
recognises.

Why? Why did you allow that evil to take you away?
But if you are tired of fighting with it, then please rest.
I would regret it if I didn't know you whole my life.
You have made it, now please rest, Mozart.

Tanawut Lex-Oudakron
Alexanders College, Woodbridge

BEST FRIEND

It all started in a morning,
I was almost late for the meeting.
Mr Lin asked me to come in,
I saw you sat on the front seat facing me,
Peered at me, saying, 'Take a seat.'
Black hair fell on your back,
You will be my best friend, I thought.

You weren't normal, you had acted some roles in some films.
No happiness, only illness.
You said you were thrown into a cold river on a cold night,
But sorry, I couldn't be your knight on that painful night.
You made a scene when you were crying like a desperado,
Cos your deadbeat dad wanted your long hair cut.
You hardly held on when your long hair had gone.
You had to leave for another plot,
With nothing but hollow in my heart.
Short hair swung behind your head.
You will still be my best friend, I thought.

I saw you again when the new year began.
I hadn't seen you for four months but we could chat like before.
Everything will get better,
You played with me like toast plays with butter.
Torturous days may not be any longer.
After graduating from junior high,
Kites went into different skies.
Long-black was all I saw,
We will always be best friends, I thought.

Shengchen Xie (15)
Alexanders College, Woodbridge

THE END OF THE WORLD AS WE KNOW IT

I know I have to get married,
I know I have to protect my family,
I know I have to treasure everything,
I know I have to study hard.
Is that enough for us?

No way, guys!
Let's keep going!

I know I have to play with my friend,
I know I have to do my homework,
I know I have to be a good person.
Is that enough for us?

I don't actually know.
But would that be the end of the world?

Michael Cheung
Alexanders College, Woodbridge

WE LEARN

It's been a long way to go.
It's hard to go through on my own.
It's suffering.
It's torturing.
My life wasn't as easy as it seems,
Without a light shining in my way,
I still keep walking on this way.
Every day we try,
We make some mistakes,
But failing isn't the cause of people becoming a failure;
Go ahead, make some mistakes!
For every time we do;
We learn,
We grow.

Puwin Chaicheewinlikit
Alexanders College, Woodbridge

THE DEATH OF WISH

I wish life wasn't a pure pain.
I wish words couldn't cut deeper than a knife.
I wish there was no darkness.
I wish there was no blindness.
I wish I hadn't tried to kill myself.
I wish, I wish, wish, wish there was no wish in my life.
I wish there was love, care and parents for me like everyone.
I wish my father hadn't stayed late at the bar,
Got home and killed my ma.
I wish there was no policeman that killed my fa.
Now I am no longer active and alive.
I wish I were there to say a thing.
'Wishing', I wish such a word didn't exist in my life.
I wished and wished that's why I am no longer there.

Mohammad Gholami
Alexanders College, Woodbridge

MY MEMORY

My memory when I was young was fear.
My memory when I was young was a friend.
I know we will meet and we will leave.
That's why I always remember you.
No matter how far apart we are,
I will always be there.
Whatever happens in the future,
I will leave it.
Even though I don't like the future,
I will always live with it.
And it could be happy or it could be sad.
But remember, it depends on you, not God.
And the future will be in my memory.

Nattida Lex-Oudakron (15)
Alexanders College, Woodbridge

HARBOUR

When I left the warm harbour,
I could always remember your caring.
When I was young,
You always taught me the truth.
When I hurt myself,
You always helped me dress the wound.
When I was in trouble,
You always helped me clean up the mess.
When I was sad,
You always comforted me.
The annual rings of the shuttle
That make your black hair change to white.

Anne Wenting
Alexanders College, Woodbridge

TODAY

There's not a cloud today, just a sky of blue,
As the sun shines bright, it feels so new.
As you walk down the street, you can see smiles from all around.
It looks like everyone has come to the town
To enjoy the summer's day and let time stand still for a little while.

Mohammed Saeed (16)
Alexanders College, Woodbridge

I COULD BE THE ONE

When the future is dark,
Maybe, I am just the white point,
Guide direction.
When the world is dark,
Maybe, I am also clean like the water.
A spring.
But who can understand my feelings, who knows,
You, him or her?
Who can be my white point or spring?
Maybe I can be the one.

Xingzeng Zheng
Alexanders College, Woodbridge

UNTITLED

Close your eyes,
Imagine cosiness,
Imagine this place where I will be understood,
Where there is no evil, no sadness,
Where you are always missed.
You would say, 'There is no place like this.'
No, there is your parents' house.

Kamila Turlykhan
Alexanders College, Woodbridge

EARTH IS OUR LIFE

Chop! Scratch! Boom!
I smelt devastation.
Stepping out the door, I sensed destruction.
In the forest, some cold-blooded people were spreading obliteration!
I saw a flood of desolation trickling through the forest.

The trumpeting of the elephants could be heard from miles away.
You could tell their pain from their noise.
The group was spreading vagrancy for millions of forest habitants!
Eek! Eek! A troop of monkeys was viewed by me swinging from branch to branch,
Trying to find shelter.
Why? Why did they not stay in their habitat?
Those heartless people cut down the monkeys' source of protection;
Used it to facilitate themselves!
How would you feel if your habitat was taken away to luxuriate someone else?

I advanced to have a closer look.
From here I could see the future of Earth.
A world with no wildlife.
A world with no attractiveness.
A world with loneliness.
A world where no one would want to be.
More and more trees were cut.
More and more habitats were being snatched away.
More and more species were dying out.

Have you ever thought carefully how it would be if the Earth fell apart?
The green, graceful skirts are being killed by our ungratefulness!
The smell of the fresh air is being turned into a cloud of pollution!
The nutritional soil is turned to ruins under our feet!
The garden of fine, fascinating flowers is fading away!
Gradually all the life on Earth will vanish!
Save the wildlife. Save the Earth!

Eliza Ali (12)
Aylesbury High School, Aylesbury

PHOBOS

Hello, dear frightened child.
Throw away your cares as I scare.
As a son of Ares, I am untamed and wild.
I am the reason you have nightmares...

Proud to say,
I'm a son of Aphrodite and Ares,
My upstart brother and I drive the magic sleigh.
Let me tell you; he is so happy- a bunch of daisies.

Don't get me started on space.
My dad is Ares, the super Greek god.
Yet he has a second face.
As Mars, the Roman god.

Me and my brother reluctantly
Have to orbit our father's second half!
The one thing we agree on, grudgingly,
Is that we hate to orbit the second half: he would laugh.

Never mistake me for my brother!
As my dear twin is just bigger and uglier!
Even though Mother
Is much lovelier.

But, I'm stuck in your head,
And now I will never be dead.
I am not a bloodshed,
I am just plain dread!

Good-scare, dear frightened child.
Remember I am the reason you have nightmares,
As a son of Ares, I am untamed and wild.
I am Phobos!

Maiurie Rasakulasuriar (12)
Aylesbury High School, Aylesbury

THE FACTIONS OF DIVERGENT

'Faction before blood'
The creators did say
And that quote is important
Even in the modern day

Abnegation the selfless
The factionless slaves
The least selfish people stay there
Or so they say

Dauntless the brave
More brave than smart
You must fight to survive
From the very start

Candor the honest
Never did tell a lie
Always telling the truth
But the truth isn't welcome all the time

Erudite the intelligent
They know everything about life
But their leader Jeanine Matthews
Caused much strife

Amity the peaceful
They abide by the law
They farm the lands
But they hate war

These are the factions
Determined by how we behave
Smart, kind, honest
Selfless and brave.

Amal Shafi (12)
Aylesbury High School, Aylesbury

OPEN YOUR EYES

You are blinded from the truth
The black silhouettes circle you silently
As you stand, unmoving, staring into blank space
It swirls around you in drifts of snow,
Encasing you inside a dome of swirling glass

Then your eyes are opened
And you can finally see the world
The moonlight shines down on you
Spread out through the icy chandeliers, curled
As if they have been wrapped around a pencil

Oh! But just look up there, what can you see?
The stars like fireworks and like twinkling diamonds
Scattered across the purple velvet sky,
Interlaced in the branches of trees silhouetted in the view
Scintillating like the ocean's surface,
Are the ice coated webs, weaving mysterious patterns

But what is that? Look over there!
They're beautiful, the mountains, cloaked in an icy veil
They loom over the glistening ocean
Threatening to overwhelm it with their shadow and sail,
Sail out into the distance

Then the silence is broken
And the wind cries out her dark tale
'It's luring you in, don't go over there!'
Your heart shouts out, it wails
You find yourself on the floor
Back in that dome of spiralling glass

And once again, you are blinded from the truth.

Zoe Amanda Chang
Aylesbury High School, Aylesbury

INSIDE OUT

The laughter pans in my head,
smiles all round
lots of hugs and sad eyes,
clinging to my face
promises never to forget them
ringing in my ear
sorrow consuming my body all together
things that hurt me,
things that make me cry,
things that give me nightmares,
things that remind me of leaving my
friends behind.
Lonely thoughts, swirling around my head
trees bowing their heads pitifully
I crash into a corner,
a dark pain consumes me
crumbling all my kindness,
threatening the ones I love
scaring myself inside out,
bringing tears to my eyes
my feet buckling beneath me
my body shivering all over
never leaving my head the
Dark thoughts within me...

Sharni Robinson
Aylesbury High School, Aylesbury

FEAR

We all meet the monster,
At some point in our lives.
It blocks out the world,
And in dark times, it thrives.

It creeps in unnoticed,
Too small to be seen,
But it grows over time,
Till it's big and it's mean.

It takes over your mind,
With its dark, twisted ways.
The more attention you give it,
The longer it stays.

It feasts on discomfort,
With a snarl and a sneer.
It has many names,
But it's best known as Fear.

Molly Squires (12)
Aylesbury High School, Aylesbury

BROKEN

I reach out to you, but you slip from my grasp
Like mist on a cold winter's night.
I'm left alone, shivering, the cold bearing into my bones,
I am broken,
Never to be repaired, I crouch, empty of love,
My heart shattering as the memories flow.
I'm abandoned, empty of joy, full of sorrow,
I am broken.

Isabelle Stringfellow (11)
Aylesbury High School, Aylesbury

SEAGULLS

S oar high in the air above everyone
E ating anything they see
A lways by the seaside
G liding over the ocean
U nited in a flock
L ike to eat fish all day
L urking around the cliffs.

Somto Okpalauko (12)
Becket Keys CE Free School, Brentwood

BEHIND THE SCENES AT BECKET KEYS

It is the end of a school day,
The students journey home to play,
The teachers gather for a meeting,
Mr Scott-Evans starts with a greeting,
Assessments, progress and plans are discussed,
Organisation is a must!

Next comes the marking; so many books!
So many frowns, so many looks,
A deep sigh: 'Oh deary me!'
They can't believe what they see.
'Oh wait a minute. It's not quite so bad.
Our teaching is working. We all should be glad!'

The morning comes round, a new day starts,
The teachers set up with hope in their hearts
For students to behave as well as can be,
To get a 9 in their GCSEs.
Coats, bags and iPhones put away,
Ready to start a brand new day.

William Tendler (13)
Becket Keys CE Free School, Brentwood

AN EVOLUTION OF POLLUTION

Earth, land, sand and the deep, blue sea
Like plants, animals could roam free,
Cavemen came and lived in harmony,
The world was the best it could be.

And then along came electricity,
A culture changing invention,
Cruel machines came and killed forestry,
Our world winced in pain but went on.

Man started demanding extra power,
Then the industries developed,
Like a lemon, the Earth turning sour,
With greenhouse effect enveloped.

Then came trains and cars, buses and planes,
Like mould, pollution filled the air,
Carbon monoxide, chemical rains,
But no one seemed to care.

Our beautiful planet is being destroyed,
Animals becoming extinct,
Loss of all creation we must avoid,
It is now time to stop and think!

Global warming and the climate's quick change,
I mean, what else is there in store?
All the magic wonders in the world's range,
Could be lost for evermore...

Rebecca Slaney (12)
Becket Keys CE Free School, Brentwood

DOGS

There are many types of dogs,
They go woof, bark and they lick,
Cocker spaniels, scotties, labradors too.
Brown, gold, white. Look at the range of wonderful colours.

We have dogs.
They are cute and that's one of the reasons we like them
But also, we know, they're man's best friend.
We know that's the truth.

I have a dog
Do you have a dog?
Mine is a mix
What type is yours?
Is your dog tall or small?
Mine is small
What type of fur does it have?
My dog is black

Dogs are like humans in a way
They need to exercise
They need to eat
They need to drink.

Zach Antoniou (12)
Becket Keys CE Free School, Brentwood

FRIENDS

Friends are there when you need them,
They're even there when you don't,
For a walk in the park,
When you're scared of the dark,
Friends are there,
Friends will care for you.

Sometimes they won't be there,
But they always care,
If you're mauled by a bear,
Chased by a hare,
Friends will be there for you.

You may not always get along,
But you will always be friends,
If you just let go,
And remember so,
Friends are there,
And they do care for you.

Charlie Major (13)
Becket Keys CE Free School, Brentwood

A NEW DAY

I opened my eyes to a brand new world,
'Good morning world!' I loudly bellowed.
I got out of bed, getting ready to dress,
But the state of me, well, I looked a mess.

I found some food and I started to eat,
To burn off the calories, I danced to the beat.
I played my games with my friends,
We fought through all the turns and the bends.

My mum started to read. Ugh, so boring,
In fact, so boring I started snoring.
My mum demanded, 'It's time for you to start reading.'
So to do it quickly, I started speeding.

Lunch, homework, video games, dinner,
After all this, I felt like a winner,
But now I'm getting some sleep for tomorrow,
Without all of this, my life would be hollow.

Euan Inverarity (13)
Becket Keys CE Free School, Brentwood

MISTAKES

When mistakes get made,
The writing fades and Tipp-Ex comes to reign.

When mistakes are made,
Friendship fades and in that time the bullies reign.

When mistakes get made,
Enemies are made, the bonds get erased.

When mistakes get made,
Aberrations are made and it's taken the wrong way.

When mistakes are made,
Some won't change but the ones who do will never fade,

Like me and you,

Because we tried.

Joshua Ryall (12)
Becket Keys CE Free School, Brentwood

THE SCARLET BEAUTY

I was a fish, drowning in his sea, since the second he smiled at me
The blue wonder in his tanzanite eyes, curved his portrait all over me.

My catalogue vision kept running around -
not landing anywhere – until he appeared
Staring with adoration, with love, with fear,
We were both in this fussy dreamy-mire.

It was that day I finally spoke to him
In my perfect dovetail and finest smile
'Je t'adore.' I looked at his crescent eyebrows over those mysterious opals,
Knowing he would give me the perfect answer.

Di-da. Di-da. Di-da.
His hesitation froze my flame
Centuries elapsed before his feathery cocoon shut;
He said he didn't like 'distractions'
He wished only to be in his own castle with vast guards
He said – he said -

'Thank you,' with his delicate voice that sliced my heart open
Gently, elegantly, devoid of all emotion
'but no.'

My scarlet lips trembled, all my blood flowed away from my heart
– completely empty whilst blistering meteors slid across my mind –
fragments splashed and – penetrated something crystal I could not feel
I was a fish drowning in the strangled air.

The beauty sleeping on the crystal bed with his scarlet lips
Once had the most resplendent eyes that resembled zircon
But the moral of the story is sinners must pay:
Destroying my scarlet passion in such a way -
Dare you not.
Thus, I punish you. For the first time,
And the last.

Keyi Yu (15)
Bellerbys College, Brighton

WHAT IF?

Have you ever said
What if?
What if I didn't run away?
What if I did?
What if I did what they asked?
What if I could go back in time change one little thing and make
everything better?

Did you ever dwell on a
What if?
What if I'd said yes?
What if I'd said no?
What if I'd done this different?
What if I'd done that different?
What if I'd done everything different what would have happened
differently?

Have you ever been scared by a
What if?
What if they come?
What if they don't?
What if I'm wrong?
What if I'm wrong?
What if the whole universe collapses in on itself because of the
decision I make?
Because of a decision you make?

What if we stopped using what ifs?
Replace what might have happened
With what did happen?
What could have been
With what was?
What I could do
With what I do?
With what you do?

What if it was that easy?

Melissa Jane Harris (14)
Bridge Learning Campus, Bristol

TOLD

When I was born, I was born a girl.
When I was born no one told me I was the weaker sex.
No one told me no matter how hard I work
I will be paid less for the same job
Just because I'm a girl.
No matter how fast I run
Or how far I throw I'm just good for a girl.
I was never told that I should never feel comfortable in my own skin
Because what I wear determines if I get raped or not.
However, it's OK to show your boobs if it's 'hot'
But not for something as natural as breast feeding.
I was never told that being 'fat' is wrong
But being 'too skinny' is bad too.
I was never told that when I grow up
And go clubbing that I can't have fun
And dance because if you put your drink down you could get drugged.
I was never told any of these things
Yet these are rules for being a girl somehow.
I had to learn. I was never told.

Abby Louise Driscol-Pike (14)
Bridge Learning Campus, Bristol

INDIVIDUAL RESPONSIBILITY

Society is responsible for the illusions of normal
Society is biased and hypocritical
Society is closed minded
Society is blamed for all of today's injustice however who
is this society?
Me, an acquaintance, strangers
You?
We blame society but we are society
And our individual responsibility is to improve our selves,
Resulting in a better society for all.

Robyn Fogg
Bridge Learning Campus, Bristol

DREAMS

'Dreams are for sleeping,' I always get told,
But wait a second let's put this craziness on hold,
Without dreams we wouldn't be complete,
Without dreams who are the new people we could meet.

Dreams are for everyone, not just you and me,
The world is full of hopes and dreams so let's accomplish them.
Keep reaching for the stars, they're closer than you know.
You could travel the world, imagine the places you'll go.

Dreams are not just for sleeping, like everyone says,
Dreams can give you the experience,
They're not just for bed.

Ignore what others say.
Without dreams the world would be dull,
Without dreams the world would be cold.
Keep dreaming, wishing and hoping on stars.
There's new adventures waiting to be told...

Courtney Bethany May Kray (14)
Bridge Learning Campus, Bristol

ONE PERSON, ONE DIFFERENCE

When it all began, it was all one person.
One difference.

One person. One difference.
One person. One existence. One life
One happiness. One love. One life saved.
One difference made.
One person could mean the world to someone.
That someone is me and that one person is Daniel James Howell.

Chloe Bradbury
Bridge Learning Campus, Bristol

THE YEAR 3000

It's a desolate land,
Left to rot and be forgotten,
Decaying buildings all around,
Lying bones left for dead,
Nuclear waste never seen,
Nobody allowed in to peek,
One man alone,
Left alive,
No help, no care,
Left to rot and decay,
Left to become bones,
And to drift into the night air,
No way to prevent this,
It will happen.
The only thing he doesn't know is when,
But there is only one problem, he cannot escape,
He needs to call help,
But how?
He has no communication with the outside world,
And so he is alone,
Left to rot and decay,
He knows that shortly,
He will be consumed
By the everlasting threat,
The nuclear waste,
That has never been seen,
Only felt,
He has to escape
And fast,
Or he will be consumed,
By the everlasting threat,
The nuclear waste,
But there is only one problem,

He cannot escape,
If he tries he will die,
Immediately,
He will die!

Eoghan Taylor (11)
Chenderit School, Banbury

THE YEAR 3000

The year 3000 a forgotten land,
Houses and buildings covered in sand,
Is the planet left to die, decaying like a rotting fly?
Then in the distance all alone,
An old man without a home,
The Earth has ended but he doesn't know,

He looks at me with an insistent stare,
The man is sinking as the world tears,
The man is vanished through the sand,
The year 3000 a forgotten land.

James Merridan (11)
Chenderit School, Banbury

SHEEP DOG

Where are you? Please don't be dead,
Why did you get shot in the head?
Please don't let me say goodbye,
I'm lost without you, please don't make me cry?

Sheep dog, sheep dog wake up,
Who put you in this state?

I can hear you
But can't respond
Please save me from my slumber

Your eyes are slowly opening,
I am seeing you awaking,

Hello my dog where were you
You gave me a fright of losing you.

Molly Gill (11)
Chenderit School, Banbury

RABBIT, RABBIT, RABBIT

Rabbit, rabbit, rabbit,
You are big, you are small,
But I've got a big one in my hall,
I love rabbits, it's a bit of a habit,
They eat carrots all day long and,
Have cuddles in the sun.

Rabbit, rabbit, rabbit,
You hop up, you hop down,
As you twitch your nose all around,
Your coat is like silk with a polka dot kilt

Rabbit, rabbit, rabbit,
You are fluffy, you are scruffy.

Olivia Smith (12)
Chenderit School, Banbury

THE RAT!

The rat was like a fly
so happy and free
also he was a wee bit sticky
his old grey feet were
soft and squidgy.

Big ones, little ones,
Fluffy ones, fat ones,
Skinny ones, long ones,
And of course stinky ones.

Lucas Barrett (11)
Chenderit School, Banbury

JACK AND JUNE

Jack and June went to the moon,
Crash landed in a crater.
Jack broke his nose and seven toes,
He's a crummy navigator.

Jack cried in pain.
June tried in vain
To soothe her injured mate.
She kissed his nose and massaged his toes
And asked him on a date.

Jack and June began to swoon,
Fell madly in love
Returned to Earth
And wed the very next day.

Hannan Dalla (12)
Featherstone High School, Southall

LIFE

Life is a puzzle.
Life is a maze.
Life is precious.
Like the memories in the back of my head.

Life could be hard.
Life could be sad.
Life could be special – could also be mad.

Life is luscious.
Life is a gear
So just be yourself and get ready for more.

More pain.
More gain.
More love
And more you.

Life is a journey
Life is life
And life will end.

So remember,
We live.
We love.
We fall,
And we rise.

However, we never fail.

Fatematez Zamifah (12)
Featherstone High School, Southall

BONFIRE NIGHT SOUP

Bring...
A bag of wood
A nip of fire
A bunch of poppers

Include...
The punch of fireworks
The smell of hot dogs
The yell of children
Then stop – no more...

Then combine it all up
And bring it all home
Spice with ginger
Include ketchup

Now let it all go cold
And serve it at night
And all that is left to do
Is invite...

Amber Louisa Huxley (12)
Featherstone High School, Southall

TIGER

Tiger creeping through the night,
in the brightness of the light.
Fire orange, solid black,
filling up her big black sack.

And there she finds a pleasant deer,
munching on the leaves real near.
She eyes her prey and lays down flat,
pounces, catches, eats, gets fat.

Lying down to have a rest,
slow digesting all her best.
Sleeping it off, having a drink,
watching the bush as the sky goes pink.

Rochelle James
Focus School Hindhead, Hindhead

SNOW

It snowed all night and all day
but the month was May.
The hills were very white
and at dawn there was a glow of light.
As I came over the hills
you could see the white mills.
The village was white
and in the blue sky there was a kite.

Jermaine Lynes
Focus School Hindhead, Hindhead

EARTH STOMPER

Tree cruncher
Earth stomper
Leaf snaffler
Water hogger.

An entertainer
Daily greeter
Giant friend
Big high seat.

I am rough and enormous
I plod as bold as a lion
As I go through the trees in the African forest
My gigantic shadow gleams like silver in the moonlight.

Alexia Critchley
Focus School Hindhead, Hindhead

THE STORM

The storm is fierce and cold,
I'm standing in a raincoat that is very old.
The rolling thunder and the bright lightning,
I can feel my heart rapidly tightening.

The storm is over, phew!
The old, damp grass is now fresh, sweet-smelling and new,
When the sun peeps through those dark clouds and shines,
We feel no longer as dark as mines.

Dani Turner
Focus School Hindhead, Hindhead

WINTER CALM

No sun, no movement,
no noise, but the hiss of solid cold.

Trees arched, branched like veins
from their trunks, their hearts.

Bushes cluster aside
the peak-iced liquorice road.

Fields surrounded; frosted like powdered sugar,
designer desert plates.

Against a misty backdrop
life suspends.

I am on hold -
at rest, peaceful, calm.

Georgie Budworth-Palmer
Hospital & Outreach Education, Northampton

ROAD THROUGH THE VALLEY

Road through the valley,
down the mountain's mouth,
where the valley lays
and the darkness shines
on this desolate road.

Up in the mountains
on a clouded night,
where is the end
of this long windy road.

Where is the motion -
not a single trace,
where is the wind
on this aggressive night.

Kain Pickering
Hospital & Outreach Education, Northampton

UNTITLED

Firefly lights the night -
A frog's tongue pulls it downward
The pond's glow fades

The fish are huddled -
A gull's beak pierces water
The school has scattered

From afar, it's sheen -
Closer, the bark is rotten
Plagued by diseases

Water grips the branch
Sundown, cool becomes colder
Frost encapsulates.

Michael Poll
Hospital & Outreach Education, Northampton

TATTOO

My skin ripping,
blood dripping.

The sharp-fast stabbing
pain of the fierce gun.

Noises make me shiver
down my spine,
'Oh well, I'll be fine.'

The tearing of skin
all over my shins
is having ink a sin?

After all, it is my skin.

Ally Lever
Hospital & Outreach Education, Northampton

MY BEACH

The soft layer of sand
of the beach.
You stare up at the dazzling blue sky,
thinking about life.
You walk along the warm sand,
hear the whisper of the wind,
the crashing waves,
up against the shore.
The sand lights up
from the brightness of the moon
and the twinkling stars
glisten in the night.

Maygan Abbott
Hospital & Outreach Education, Northampton

EXCITEMENT

Excitement is purple!
It tastes like Haribo sweeties
And smells like a bath-bomb shop
Excitement looks like dreams coming true
And sounds like children squealing
It gives me a rush through my body.

Gabby Mouzo (12)
King's Rochester Preparatory School, Rochester

NOVA BEAST

I am Nova,
Powerful and furious
I soar through the skies
like an eagle
up high

I caused the Big Bang
it was when I whispered to
your nan

The sun is my baby cousin
I saw him born
he was born yesterday

I am Nova

I am watching you right now
you will never see me
I am living and getting stronger at the same time
I will live forever
If I shout I can destroy the Milky Way
when I scream what happens is beyond your belief

I am Nova
I heard your cry
when you were born

I hear every last gasp for breath as someone dies
but I also hear the wailing of every newborn baby
when I listen to every bullet in a gun being fired I get angry

Earthquakes happen and global pandemics happen,
that's terrible
if I go in a rage some animals become extinct
how do you think the dinosaurs went extinct?

I am Nova
if you see me it means it is time for
the end.

Temi Lasekan (12)
King's Rochester Preparatory School, Rochester

I AM JAGER

I have seen the world
But so much more
I have seen stars
So bright!

I have seen beings
Fall to dust.
I have seen the sun
Rise and fall.

I have seen the world
Fall into nothing.
I have seen everything
Come and go.

I have heard screams
Fade from life.
I have heard bangs
As great as life

I have heard the waves
Lapping against the shore.
I have heard everything
Come and go.

I was once a grain of sand
Staring at the sun
I was once a pencil
A humble writing instrument.

I was once whole planets
And sometimes just a cell
I have witnessed the Big Bang
In fact, I am the Big Bang.

I know secrets so dark
And things waiting to happen
I know why water gushes

Waves lap
Clocks tick
And people scream.

I know, I have heard, I have seen and been everything possible
I am Jager.

Luke Harald Peter Stringer (12)
King's Rochester Preparatory School, Rochester

THE NOT SO FRIENDLY FRIENDS

I just don't seem to get it
But I'd really like to bet it
Why some people hate to see you win.
They stand there and all cheer
But then when you're not so near
They act as if they never ever said it!

They seem to be your friend
And stick with you to the end
But get jealous at the very smallest thing.
We are all at school together and in teams play hell for leather
So why can't all of us be celebrating?

As a team we should encourage
And not try to discourage,
Our triumphs on and off the court.
So next time we line up to try to win the cup
Let's remember that we are all the best at sport.

So when I win my match, shout, 'Well done,' and clap
And let's all be proud of what we have done,
As next time it's your turn and the honours you have earned
I'll make sure that you're the special one!

Amelia Dobson (12)
King's Rochester Preparatory School, Rochester

TAIKAN

I am creation
I know the meaning of life
Time runs through my fingers
Like a drop of water

I have seen the last dinosaur
Take its final breath
I have lived among them
My body has taken many forms
I have lost count

I have been a plant
A land and sea creature
Don't forget the sky
Its wide variety of colours

I know how many grains of sand
There are in the Sahara
I know the answer to the question
Is there life out there

I am God's best friend
I have seen Atlantis sink below the icy waters
I played the iceberg in Titanic
I was in the Big Bang

I have seen you sleep
I was watching you through the window
Your bed was so comfortable
And then you said in your dream, 'Bingo!'

I am Mother Nature
When you make me angry
A storm erupts
When I am happy
The sun shines.

I am Taikan!

Edward Hyde (12)
King's Rochester Preparatory School, Rochester

UNTITLED

I come from a house of waiting forever
Waiting for Dad to come home
For tasty food, perfect posture
Bed at nine sharp

I come from woofs and miaows
Jet-black noses and purring so soft
Furry faces and wagging tails
Smelly food and dry biscuits

I come from the Oxford dictionary
Maths tutors and homework
Singing day in, day out
Getting home at 6.30 Tuesday, Thursday, Friday

I come from happiness
Practising piano and French horn
Lessons every week
Practising half an hour each

I come from hot, happy holidays
Eight weeks at most
Swimming pools and seaside lunches
Ice lollies that melt far too quickly

I come from family time
Opening presents and watching Christmas TV
Having Christmas dinner
Repeat again for Boxing Day

I come from my friends
Always there for me
James, Jude, Luke and Phoebe, just some of their names

I come from loving parents
Who care for me
Who love me no matter what.

Oliver Davis (12)
King's Rochester Preparatory School, Rochester

PINK

Pink is a soft creamy cake, sparkling and glittering so brilliantly bright, it's like a star reflecting in the lustre of the night light.

The pink rose that's reddened by the sun, coral in the shade like a face flushed warm with fun from a run.
The candyfloss clouds all over the sky so pretty it makes me sigh.

It's so beautiful that it glistens so bright, it makes me feel so warm inside.
The smile on your lips, the colour of your skin, the warmth of your heart close to mine.

You're all around me so warm and full of love, you've opened my eyes, filled my heart and with you always by my side I will never need to hide.

It smells of joy, so much pleasure and happiness as it beats so fast, so full of love it's going so fast I may even break into a blush.

It looks like a flamingo fluttering its gorgeous wings around, so bright, so crimson, so much fun to be around.

It's the blush of a cheek, a face full of colour, an embarrassing moment that you haven't chosen to respond to and now you need to recover.
A moment in time captured in colour, it happens all the time to my face when it flutters.

When I'm feeling alone I look up to the sky and watch the flashes of light that flicker so bright from behind the clouds they shine full of life. They light up the sky like magnificent fireworks so late into the night. And then I don't feel alone anymore.

It tastes of freedom, it feels so relaxing, it sounds like a bedtime story being played over and over
Soothing my ears, relaxing my mind, I'm closing my eyes.

Harry Wadhams (11)
King's Rochester Preparatory School, Rochester

THE GIANT FLYING MACHINE

I'm off! Embracing the elements,
In the giant flying machine.
Soaring past eagles, gulls and falcons,
In the giant flying machine.
Twisting, turning, swooping, diving,
In the giant flying machine.
Feeling the air tugging at me,
In the giant flying machine.
Gazing at hills, streams and valleys,
In the giant flying machine.
Feeling the wind bite into me,
In the giant flying machine.
Feeling sudden lurching,
In the giant flying machine.
Hearing the twang of ropes failing,
In the giant flying machine.
Feeling the G-force grip me,
In the giant flying machine.
Plunging, twisting, turning, falling,
In the giant flying machine.
Screaming my fear to the sky,
In the giant flying machine.
Sea and sky the wrong way round,
In the giant flying machine.
Feeling the water grip me,
In the giant flying machine.
Descending through the briny depths,
In the giant flying machine.
Now at rest amongst the kelp,
Me and my giant flying machine.

Rupert Walker (13)
King's Rochester Preparatory School, Rochester

INSECURITY

Am I fat like a pig in its gestation period?
Am I too thin?
Am I too small, forever feeling inferior and having to look up at
people?
Am I a giant that intimidates everyone and knocks everything over?
Or am I just plain ugly?

Am I a walking acne machine that could donate spots to a cheetah?
Or is my face too big?
Do my legs look like the forestation of the Amazon?
Or am I just plain ugly?

Do I have radiant blue eyes that glisten like the sun in all its glory?
Do I have a shapely body?
Or do I take after a caveman in its prime?
Or is it time that I said, 'Or am I just plain ugly?'

Do I avoid mirrors as if they were the Black Death?
And glower at those who admire their own bodies.

When did I stop and take time
To appreciate me for who I am?
Not by the number of my vexing moon crater or dust particle sized
spots
Not even my social importance
Just me

Some day boys and girls will see that they will always be 'me'
Whether thought to be aesthetically pleasing or not
Hold your head up high and parade like you know that you look just
fine.

Buyikunmi Ajayi (13)
King's Rochester Preparatory School, Rochester

PAST AND PRESENT

I come from a city with a square shaped cathedral,
left as a baby for a new abode.
My parents' ambition brought them southwards
settling in the town I now know.
I come from a town which is on a main line,
with speedy trains Channel bound,
whizzing and buzzing flashing past
making a special whooshing sound.
I come from a house which had two cats
squabbling and playing every day
but one got hit by a careless car
and now, *crash*, has no pal to play.
I come from a home with loving grandparents
who support me in so many ways,
fetching and carrying and watching like guards.
I enjoy going to my new school after my old one
where I spent happy days
as Head Boy there and an 11+ passer
sporty too in every way.
I intend to work as hard as I can
to make those who love me very proud.
I come from a family with five uncles
who work as busily as bees
(one of whom is a lazy toad!)
my mum and dad have stressful jobs too
working long hours and travelling far.
It means we have a lovely car!

James Watkins (12)
King's Rochester Preparatory School, Rochester

DREAMS

Some dream big,
Some dream small,
Many will achieve, many will fall.

Whatever it is,
Wait for your chance,
Graduation or a victory dance.

Dream of...
Being a doctor, that will heal the sick,
Or play for England with a hockey stick.

You may come across hurdles,
That will be difficult to jump,
But just keep striving and don't get the hump.

To achieve that dream,
You need to work hard,
Remembering not to get a red card.

Turn your dream into reality,
It is pointless just dreaming,
Cheer on your mates but not just screaming.

When the time is right,
That moment will be sweet,
On top of the podium, wouldn't that be neat!

Be a good team player,
And don't let them down,
If you follow these rules, you will get the crown.

Emily-Jane Victoria Godden (13)
King's Rochester Preparatory School, Rochester

I AM FORTUNIA

I have seen
All of the glistening
Golden
Brightly smiling stars
Spring to life
In the thick
Black sky above

I have heard
The angelic
Soft
Twinkling
Patter of
A fairy's feet
On my
Silk, springy
Feather pillow

I know the
Strange
Mystical
Dramatic
Happenings
That are yet to come
Hurtling
Towards the Earth.

I am Fortunia.

Lily Sheppard (12)
King's Rochester Preparatory School, Rochester

THE FUTURE

In the future, what new tech will there be?
Amazing devices for everyone to see.
Will everyone have flying cars?
Or will humans all be living on Mars?

Will animals finally learn how to talk?
Or will humans use rocket boots so we don't have to walk?
Maybe there'll be shoes that are fast like a rocket,
Maybe there'll be mini robots that you can keep in your pocket.

Will human and robots live together?
Or will there be a way to control the weather?
In the future, what new tech will there be?
Amazing devices for everyone to see.

Will someone find a way to change the law?
Or will robots and humans go to war?
Will robots finally take over the Earth?
Or will all animals learn how to surf?

Will humans gain super powers?
Or will there be man-eating flowers?
Will humans finally learn how to fly?
Soaring in the air, in the light blue sky.

Will the earth be destroyed by a meteorite?
Or will animals learn how to fly a kite?
In the future, what new tech will there be?
So lets just wait, find out and see.

Jonathan Pedro (12)
King's Rochester Preparatory School, Rochester

THE FUTURE

The future, the future, what is it like?
I wish I could go there, just get on my bike.
There must be something that beholds the truth,
I suppose, to find out, I could be like a sleuth.

There must be something out there, which stores my dreams.
No, not my mind you silly person, something else it seems.
I'm sorry, it's hard to explain what I think.
It's just that I had a feeling but I think it's started to shrink.

I had a thought ever since I was young,
But please don't leave because the story isn't done.
I've always thought that something is waiting for me,
I don't know what, where or why but there is something,
there must be.

I dreamt that in the future everything would be tech.
From lightsabers to sofas but so far these haven't been met.
I thought there was so much more,
Until the economy went into downpour.

I dream of being a scientist but I don't know if I'm a bit of an optimist.
I dream to change the world one day... for the better.
But all the world has done in three things is: revolution, pollution
and domination.
So how is this going to help in the future, in the future, the future?

Marcus Roe (13)
King's Rochester Preparatory School, Rochester

WAR – SOLDIERS

It is dark and cold and soldiers are tired
But they can't rest because they are fighting
Always thinking about their families
Even if they wish to, they can't stop

Trying to keep everyone's hopes up
Soldiers upset and can't get enough sleep
Trenches are muddy and wet and deep
Even if they wish to, they can't stop

Soldiers dying, it is upsetting
Nothing can stop it from happening
Soldiers upset, in distress
Even if they wish to, they can't stop

The time has come to leave their friends behind
It is sad but exciting to see their families
But everyone is distraught over everything
Even if they wish to, they can't stop

All of the field covered in blood and corpses
Is disturbing and disgusting
But what they did for us was astonishing
And we will never forget
Even if they wish to, they can't stop.

Ashvinder Sahota (13)
King's Rochester Preparatory School, Rochester

BLUE

Blue is the colour of calmness
Like the deep blue sea against the golden sand on a sunny beach
Calmness is the view of a sun setting, leaving the sky a pinky-orange
Watching the day fade away and all your worries and stress with it
Calmness is like starting afresh and beginning again
Blue is like melodic music playing in the background helping
you forget.

Louise Billingsley-Griffin
King's Rochester Preparatory School, Rochester

TIREDNESS

When you're tired you can't think straight,
You struggle through the day.
You often lose your sense of time,
And you can't get thoughts to stay.

You often laugh at normal things
And cry at the slightest pains.
You might find you become more aware,
Of all the minor strains.

It's something you can see in others,
Being deprived of sleep.
It's something nobody likes to be,
It almost makes one weep.

So what is there to be done about,
This spiral of numbing fatigue?
This ghastly and alien feeling,
That knocks me out of my league.

Dad always has the answer,
Although he knows there'll be a fight.
He'll nearly always insist upon,
The shame of an early night.

Archie Caithness (13)
King's Rochester Preparatory School, Rochester

HATE!

I have blue eyes and
smooth skin and I hiss in
my cage, waiting for
people to feed me.
Give me food – I hate
people – I hate anybody
who doesn't feed me.

Harrison Toby Fermor (12)
King's Rochester Preparatory School, Rochester

EMOTIONS

Hate is dark blue,
It tastes like toast that is out-of-date
And smells rusty and old.
Hate sounds like a demon screaming.
Hate looks like a mean and abandoned house.

Love is bright red,
It tastes like a fresh strawberry
And smells clean and new.
Love looks like the king of Valentine's Day.
Love looks bright like a sunset.

Sadness is grey.
It tastes unknown
And smells like the happiness has left.
It sounds like Death's poem.
Sadness looks down like gloomy rain.

Happiness is bright orange,
It tastes like a pea
And smells of growing dandelions.
Happiness looks fun like a new playground.

Benedict Way (12)
King's Rochester Preparatory School, Rochester

MELANCHOLY

Melancholy, I feel not in the city of gold but the city of blue
Who is friend? Who is foe? Who is a stranger? Who do I know?
I feel not like a bird but grace in the earth
I feel like crying but no tear will shed

My body a prison, I'm sick in bed
All of my emotions they feel so dead
Finally a tear has shed all of my emotions
I feel they have fled but they are all in my head

I have no reason – I feel like I've committed some treason.

Robert Humphris (13)
King's Rochester Preparatory School, Rochester

UNTITLED

I come from a town
Crammed with houses
High and low
I come from
A house of books
Dad's collection of medical texts
Filling the shelves
I come from a household
Where it's very cold
Ice white walls
Attract all
I come from a city
It's very pretty
Lots of kitties
In London, the city
I come from a place
Just in case
It's like a base
In a race
To be the best.

Yasir Hafeez (13)
King's Rochester Preparatory School, Rochester

THE INCENSED MUTANT

I am stalking you,
I have been travelling all day and I have not
Tasted a single drop of blood since yesterday.
I am on the top of the van,
Ready to pounce on you.
I have waited to suck your blood,
But first, I will wrap you in my web,
Then I will have you.
Ha ha ha ha!
I will be expecting you...

Tatenda Madyiwa (13)
King's Rochester Preparatory School, Rochester

121

I COME FROM

I come from a gate,
A gate that never leaves my side,
I come from a black hole,
This black hole wanders the universe in an eternal stroll.

I come from a turtle,
On this turtle are four elephants,
On these four elephants is a diamond,
In this diamond is a world,
That's the world I come from.

I come from a wonderland,
This wonderland consists of all the beauties, horrors and wonders of
the world,
Each of those features make up the world,
This world is the place I come from.

I come from a planet,
This planet has over seven billion people in it,
This planet's secret is yet to be revealed,
Because this planet is Planet Earth...

David Oluwadurotimi Adebanjo (13)
King's Rochester Preparatory School, Rochester

I COME FROM

I come from the sound of barking in the garden,
Which is drowned out by the busy road,
I come from a book in which I lose myself,
Imagining that I am part of it.

I come from a heart-warming, sweet dog
Who jumps into my arms as soon as I come home.
I come from a teenage brother
Who talks with a so-called enthusiastic shrug of the shoulder.
I come from a mad house
Mad, mad, mad!

Amy Osborne (13)
King's Rochester Preparatory School, Rochester

I COME FROM

I come from a planet called Earth
It is blue and green and is teeming with life
Unlike Mars, which is raging red
Which is, perhaps, a warning of death.

I come from a world that I would like to say is:
Free of wars and free of hate
Where the ocean whirls and splashes until it meets the soft sand
The movement of the tide is like the heartbeat of the land

I come from a country where the seasons
Turn colours from green to gold
Waving yellow daffodils in the springtime
And crisp white snow underfoot in winter.

I come from a house
Where we play and have fun
the hamster wheel spins and almost takes flight
A place where the sound of music has always filled my ears
Here, I am safe from a world full of war and hate.

George Crawford (12)
King's Rochester Preparatory School, Rochester

I COME FROM

I come from a sleepy village
Surrounded by tall trees
And bustling motorways.

I come from a red garden gate,
A winding path and a red door.

I come from an Alaskan malamute
As big as an elephant
With a giraffe's tongue
It devours all of the food
Its giant eyes can see through things
Always eyeing up the food.

Dylan Richmond (13)
King's Rochester Preparatory School, Rochester

123

EARTH SONG

A spray of water,
A mountainous peak,
The wind plays a song
When the Earth starts to speak.

An old shallow rock,
A river's loud roar,
Creates a new tune
That plays on the shore.

A tree's hollow soul,
A flower's new sight,
Brings home an ending
And a start to the night.

The stars' wicked glow,
A moon that shines bright,
A sad lullaby
That tells you goodnight.

Aidan Richardson (12)
King's Rochester Preparatory School, Rochester

UNTITLED

Let us remember the fallen soldiers
Who fought for our freedom
Let us salute the soldiers
Who lay in the flag draped coffins

Let us think of the soldiers who lay beneath those unmarked graves
What person lies beneath them
Let us recollect the young age of the soldiers
Who spent most time in trenches

Let us wear our poppies with pride
To remember the loved ones who did not survive
Let us tell the next generation
Don't let them be forgotten.

Tegan Wimble (13)
King's Rochester Preparatory School, Rochester

WHAT DO YOU DO ON THE LOO?

What do you do when you're on the loo?
Do you read the newspaper
Or do you watch funny videos of puppies on YouTube?

When you're on the loo, do you get on with it
Or drag it out so that you don't have to do your homework?

When do you do it?
When you're just about to go to bed to stay up later
Or in the morning ready for the day ahead?

Do you go when you want to catch up on TV by yourself
Or just think about the world and see what difference you
could make?

Do you fall asleep or stay awake?
Do you watch 'Take Me Out' or 'Britain's Got Talent'?

Some people like to listen to music but what about you?
What do you do on the loo?

George Taylor (12)
King's Rochester Preparatory School, Rochester

THE FUTURE

The future is like weather, always unpredictable
The future is a similar definition to life: you never know what you're
going to get
The future is time, it is never-ending
The future can pass quickly, try not to regret anything
The future can be quick
The future can be short, it all depends on what you make it
The future is cruel, you can't go back to undo a mistake
The future cannot be trusted, it is not man's best friend
The future can be tomorrow, the future can be next week
The future can be next month, the future can be next year
The future is not set in stone, so make it a good one
The future has arrived.

Pedro Moniz Gomes (12)
King's Rochester Preparatory School, Rochester

KHANIVORE

I am the Khanivore.
I have seen the last dinosaur being wiped off this Earth,
I have seen the Big Bang implode, then explode,
I have seen creation,
I have seen other worlds.

I have heard the saddest cries,
I have heard birdsong echoing in the mountains,
I have heard the deafening roar of armies ready to fight,
I have heard the secret of Atlantis' location.

I know all secrets, all bribes, all crimes,
I know more than any God known to primitive mankind,
I know why the humming bird flies backwards.

I know what you will do tomorrow,
And the next day, and the day after...

I am the Khanivore!

Jamie Skitt (11)
King's Rochester Preparatory School, Rochester

UNTITLED

Black is fear, a rotten, small, lacking heart inside the Devil
Fear is like a boy in a pitch-black room being tortured
It is a shadow of Hades
It feels like a vampire sucking the happiness out and leaving a bad memory
It tastes like a rotten apple
It looks like nothing!
And is a quiet as nothing!

Anger is the colour of red
It is as furious as losing and tastes of danger
Anger feels like a wrecking ball
It looks like bulls
It feels like danger.

Frederick Way (12)
King's Rochester Preparatory School, Rochester

CROMOS THE ALL POWERFUL

I am Cromos the all-powerful...
I have seen the ferocious teeth of a dinosaur
I have seen the wonders of Jesus healing a blind man
I have seen the apple that dropped on Isaac Newton's head
And I have seen the victory of every war
I have heard the loudest sound from the big bang
I have heard the fearsome battle cry of the Vikings
I have heard the impact from when the Titanic crashed into the iceberg
And I have heard the first laugh of every single baby.
I know the reason that humans exist
I know the whereabouts of all other life in the universe
I know the emotions of every human being
And I can see ten seconds into the future.
I am Cromos
Don't ever think you're alone.

Callum MacDonald (12)
King's Rochester Preparatory School, Rochester

I COME FROM

I come from an Irish family.
Who get excited when the rugby is on.
Guinness is everywhere,
And language shall not be repeated.

I come from a family with a West Highland terrier,
Who jumps up when I come home from school.
He comes from an Irish family, his name is Tayto!

I come from a crazy family,
Having three siblings is mad.
I come from supporting parents,
My mum makes me cry with laughter every day,
And my dad is hard at work all day,
But likes to mess around once in a while.

Maria Aisling Tooher (13)
King's Rochester Preparatory School, Rochester

127

I AM REPSECON

I am Repsecon

I have seen the light of day
I saw the dinosaurs roam this Earth like giants
I have seen the world become a better place
I saw the first star form.

I have heard the first baby cry
I heard the last dinosaur gasp for air
I have heard all your deepest secrets
I have heard the curses of ancient Egypt

I know how many grains of sand are in the Sahara
I was the iceberg that the Titanic hit
I was once the bombs that killed the Germans
I was once the sun that warmed this Earth.

I am Repsecon.

Alice Moody (12)
King's Rochester Preparatory School, Rochester

I'M SORRY I ATE YOUR CHOCOLATE

I have eaten
the chocolate
that you
bought yourself the other day

and which
I knew I wasn't
meant to eat
without you knowing, today.

I'm sorry
it was yummy
I will buy you
another one someday.

Alice Overend (12)
King's Rochester Preparatory School, Rochester

THE FUTURE

In the future what gadgets will there be?
Amazing things for everyone to see.
Will there be robot wars?
Or will there be floating carpets on the floor?
Will we have special shoes?
Will dogs do floating poos?
As for where I'll be
I don't know where
The future is waiting somewhere for me
Will humans and robots live together?
Will Earth still stay here forever?
Will aliens start doing the Olympics?
Or will gorillas start taking cool pics?
The future is a mystery
Let's solve it together, just you and me.

Zackary Immanuel (12)
King's Rochester Preparatory School, Rochester

KNOCK, KNOCK, DRIP, DROP

Knock, knock
Is anyone there?

Knock, knock
Drip, drop
Is anyone there?

Knock, knock
Drip, drop
Stamp, stamp
Is anyone there?

Silence

Knock, knock.

Imogen Llewellyn-MacDuff (12)
King's Rochester Preparatory School, Rochester

UNTITLED

Will gadgets be no more
Or will aliens take over?
Will robots replace us
Or will there be teleporting?
Is there going to be the Olympics
Or are we going to be living on Mars
Or will we be in bars?
Will there be exotic foods
Or terrible flus?
Will we sound like fools
Or shop in malls
Or will there be animals?

Rowhan Basi (11)
King's Rochester Preparatory School, Rochester

SLUGS

Slugs are slow.
You could drink a cup of joe.
Before the slug would go,
You could watch it for days,
But you might get a bit dazed.
It has no pace,
It would lose the race.
Don't bet your money.
On the slow little sluggy;
You will lose your money,
And you will feel bad in the tummy.
The poor little slug.

Sam Nash (12)
King's Rochester Preparatory School, Rochester

THIS IS JUST TO SAY

I have worn
The brand new socks
That were in your shopping bag

And which
You were probably
Going to wear
To the wedding.

Forgive me.
They were perfect
So delicate
And soft.

Sam Gill (12)
King's Rochester Preparatory School, Rochester

I COME FROM

I come from a dark cave in a scary mountain
Where a blind bat with wings like a swan
And a bald head leaves scratches on the walls

I come from the bang of a gun
That drowns out the screaming of death
And the never-ending cries of war
And the click of a reload

I come from the roar of a plane
Ready to leave the country
That drowns out the whining of machines
And the sorrow of a bird getting sucked into the turbine.

Aron Gabriel Dencker (12)
King's Rochester Preparatory School, Rochester

I COME FROM

I come from a house on a noisy street
Where a large, affectionate dog
With golden fur coat licks your whole face!

I come from a home where BBC Radio 2 blasts
And the TV is as loud as thunder!

I come from a large garden, where
Foxes majestically run as fast as planes
Where the birds tweet early in the morning.

I come from a smelly garage
Of sweaty workout machines
And large spiders crawling around.

I come from smelly socks
Left lying around for other people to pick up!

I come from a small bedroom
Where books are piled upon the bookshelf.

I come from a road
With a mini roundabout
Where you hear *screech!*

I come from a trainline
Where all the trains
Are delayed for 'works'.

William Gaisford-St. Lawrence (12)
King's Rochester Preparatory School, Rochester

I COME FROM

I come from a town
As loud as an explosion
Busy roads, talkative people, large houses
Made out of skin coloured bricks
I come from loud voices, bowls of jollof rice and rice with fish soup
Plates with chips, wedges and chicken with ketchup,
Chicken noodles, spaghetti Bolognese and lasagne
I come from a house of musicians, YouTubers, singers,
Gamers and a brother who hardly ever cleans up his room.
Tall people and a brother who should have left for college
five weeks ago!

Temidayo Sofowora (13)
King's Rochester Preparatory School, Rochester

UNTITLED

Death is black, like the cloak of the Grim Reaper
Death feels like saying goodbye to something you love
It smells like rich, out of date egg
It tastes like a horrible, rotten, dead animal
And it is the sound of the last breath a person will ever take.

Pain is red, like the blood of your wound
Pain feels like a stab in your life with a knife
It smells like the blood from a murder
It tastes like something dying inside of you
And it is the sound of your body screaming in your head.

Xavier Smitherman-Cairns (13)
King's Rochester Preparatory School, Rochester

133

SECRETS OF THE JUNGLE AT NIGHT

Twigs snap, crackle
Shattering the silence of the night
Alligators on the banks of the stream
Slide through the mud to the depth below
Lazy buffaloes wallow in the squishing, oozing mud
On the bank of the nearby swamp
Out where the river glides
Sullen, deep and slow.

The river glides through the jungle like an artery
Sustaining the life that depends on it
Trailing creepers twist and twine
Creating dark shadows against the white moonlight
Parrots camp for the night
Out where the river glides
Sullen, deep and slow.

Suddenly a tiger's thunderous roar
Makes the world aware
Of the wild and weird that is here
Hunters and the hunted living side by side
Lazily wallowing buffaloes buried to nose and throat
Move quickly away from the floating death
Out where the river glides
Sullen, deep and slow.

The lush jungle, the coarse cane grasses
Of the African plains
Nourished by the tropical rain
Glistens in the moonlight
Casting a drowsy magical spell
Out where the river glides
Sullen, deep and slow.

On the banks of the river
Where the gazelle grave
The cranes fly to their nests in the reed beds
Against the dark evening sky
Hiding in the jungle's dark, damp embrace
In the darkness of the tropical night
Out where the river glides
Sullen, deep and slow.

Noor Adam Kazi (12)
King's Rochester Preparatory School, Rochester

THE RIVER

The river of sadness slips
Away from the patch of laughter
Like a bird lost in the confusion of life.

The river of resentment rears
Away from the land of calm and comfort
Like a knife tearing through hearts.

Scarlett Noraika (12)
King's Rochester Preparatory School, Rochester

TREE

If you think about it really hard, a tree can tell a good story.
You are the tree and your friends and family are the leaves.
Sometimes you get along with them well but every one is going to fall out at some point
You lose all your leaves but they always come back
Because at the end of the day you can't do much without them.

Sophie West (12)
King's Rochester Preparatory School, Rochester

DISGUST

Disgust is green
It tastes like snot
And smells like rotten eggs
It looks like a moldy orange
And sounds like a burp
It makes me want to be sick!

Tom Byrne (12)
King's Rochester Preparatory School, Rochester

THE WORLD I AM IN

The world I'm in
Is the world I will never escape,
Though
I wish I could.
I've had enough of the dark sky,
Staring down at me each morning.
I hate being the only person who can smile.
Sadness is the new happy;
Happy no longer exists.
We all live in dark houses.
People are always working, never having fun.
In most people's brains,
Names of bright colours aren't in their vocabulary.
I do wish I could escape this place,
But deep
Down,
I know I never will.

Tabi Arnfeld (12)
Langtree Academy, Reading

WHO AM I

Who am I?
I am me and me am I.
I'm a girl, not a boy, and that's what I am!
A sister,
and a daughter,
and lots of other things.
How about you?
I'd love to hear something:
A girl, or a boy,
A pink, or a blue.
I wonder, I wonder...
Who
or what
are you?

Polly Keene (12)
Langtree Academy, Reading

MY FUTURE

For me, my future will be great!
It's fun, not bad; light, not grey.
My jobs, for one, they must be fun,
Like giving post to everyone!
A builder too – that one sounds great -
Or making chairs and tables for my mates.
There's one more thing on my list of three:
A plasterer I'd like to be.
I'll mold some things just like my daddy.
There is just one more thing I'd like to do,
And that's spend time with my family too!
That is all my life has planned;
I hope it's just as I command.

Izzy Byron (11)
Langtree Academy, Reading

A DEAD CITY

I
Am
Far
From
Home.
Seeing
Mankind
Shadowed
From evils
Their paths
Of ruination
Follow them to
Their homes and
Cities. My heart
was far from home.
My heart was broken.
My heart was crushed.

Hannah Osborne (11)
Mascalls School, Tonbridge

THE ZOMBIE POLAR BEAR ENCOUNTER

The pitch-black eyes
Staring through my soul
Its rouge bloodstained fur
Was a rose waiting to be picked
Its achromatic broken bones
Stained with the blood of its kills
Its crinkled fur
Made it look as though I was its next victim, or was I?
The brainless beast was a master of slaughter and torture.

Ashley Dylan Bissell (14)
Mascalls School, Tonbridge

RISE

O
To
The
Dead
I shall
Praise
With the
Power so
Tempting
They shall
Journey back
Bringing pain
And sorrow
As they rise.

Josh Kemp (11)
Mascalls School, Tonbridge

EYES IN THE SKY

I
Wished upon
A yellow star
It was as bright
As it could be, I
Knew it was a loved one
Because I thought it winked at me.

Grace Murley (11)
Mascalls School, Tonbridge

MY UTOPIA

As
I walked
Into my utopia,
All I could see
Were birds flying high, they
Were very pretty and colourful also
They were singing very loudly and peacefully
The butterflies flew through the air, what a
Gentle meander, tigers growling, scaring them off they scampered
I heard a grumble in a bush, I wondered what
I was going to walk into. I carried on walking in
I entered sheepishly but it was the end of my journey through
My utopia. I had to say a sad goodbye; I had a wonderful
Time. I walked home, it was long and tiring, I hoped to survive.

Alice Beach (11)
Mascalls School, Tonbridge

MY FORTHCOMING DAYS

As I walk into my utopia I found
Saplings, shrubs and a futuristic city
Growing with bright colours.
A man in this city chomps, no food but KFC.
This man works at a shop,
This shop puts coins in a till as civilians pass him coins.
This man has a futuristic floating car
Nobody thinks of 'e' now,
Thnx to txting.

Jack Nightingale (12)
Mascalls School, Tonbridge

SONNET TO CANDYFLOSS

Candyfloss you are as sweet as cake
You are as pink as the Pink Panther
You are not all that easy to make
so buying you is the answer
You are given to me on a stick
Or sometimes you can be in a bag
Both are good to bite or to lick
but too much will always make you gag
Your taste is always really nice
Unlike tiny deep-fried mice.

Kai Cozens (12)
Notton House School, Chippenham

BISCUIT IN THE MOONLIGHT

Biscuit on a picnic,
Biscuit on a bus,
Biscuit on a blanket,
Biscuits just for us.

Biscuit dogs are barking,
Biscuit stars are bright,
Biscuit cars are parking,
Biscuit moonlit night.

Klavell Wilson (13)
Notton House School, Chippenham

MY BULLYING

It's painful, they make you feel like an annoying itch,
All the boys and girls in class calling you a snitch
But most of the time they call you the worst stuff.
Especially you and your mum being the targets of cusses (and many don't even know her!)
Saying bad things about your family and saying that your family don't love you, causing you to be left biting your lip and in a huff and puff.
Your anguish and hurt instantly bubbles and boils inside,
Even just thinking about it you blink back those tears,
But those emotions just keep building up and that you cannot hide,
They trick you into having not only them,
But yourself you'll despise,
And making you think being different to them is an aspect of yourself,
You need to hide,
And think all that matters is your...
Coolness,
Stupidity,
Wildness,
Popularity,
Badness,
Rudeness, phone, figure and size
It's pathetic, you are pathetic, they make you feel pathetic,
The fact that you haven't done anything about it is pathetic,
All the witnesses in class not telling anyone about it is pathetic,
The advice on the Internet is useless and pathetic,
your parents not knowing or being concerned about your change in behaviour,
Or only realising you're hurting and beat around the bush,
Is... is... it's... just pathetic!
Time ticks over so slowly after waking up at midnight due to the worst of the nightmares every Sunday,
Dreading to start school all over again but I know I have to anyway.

Cecile Kwarteng (12)
Oasis Academy Hadley, Enfield

143

A SPELL TO TELL THE PAST, PRESENT AND FUTURE

Now and then
Today and tomorrow
Full of pain, death and sorrow

A gleaming ray from a dying sun
The last scream from a dead man's tongue
Yesterday's birth
Tomorrow's death
Soon there will be nothing left

Now and then
Today and tomorrow
Full of pain, death and sorrow

The last creak of a dying tree
For now you are but you won't be
Pain is eternal, you are not
Your death will come doubt me not
For soon, for soon you will be free
So come, so come, so come to me

Now and then
Today and tomorrow
Full of pain, death and sorrow

Past and present I see thee
I see the darkness coming to me
The future is dark
As dark as night
To all of us come
The very bright light

Now and then
Today and tomorrow
Full of pain, death and sorrow.

Seth Luxton (12)
Okehampton College, Okehampton

CHRISTMAS IN THE TRENCHES

Candles rise above the frozen trench,
Confusion covers the French,
Grabbing our guns,
A sweet hymn warms the night,
Our guns sat down.

We sing too,
Singing the night away,
Men sleep in peace:
No guns shouting,
No men approaching.

The smell of the non-violent morning,
The cold but ever so warming covered death,
No sound. No violence. No perishing.
A man approaches us;
Guns stand in fear.

He holds his hands up in fear,
We place our guns down but still with our fingers.
He is shaking like a tree in the wind.
Brave man; brave heart.
We step into death terrified of the unknown.

A ball flies, not a shell but a football,
Smiles and laughter,
Goals after goals,
Greetings after greetings,
Tackles after tackles.

The sound of a gun.
We turn our backs on the beautiful sun,
Into the trench.
The war is back,
Just like that.

Billy Mann (12)
Okehampton College, Okehampton

LIVING BY INCHES

The rain, merciless, relentless,
Fills our trench,
The water level
Just inches from our knees.

We are told to get ready,
That soon we will go over the top,
Into No-Man's-Land which lies,
Just inches before us.

Lying,
Chilled to the bone,
Bullets whizzing above,
Inches from our heads.

The call comes,
Soon we will go,
For we are surely now,
Inches from our death.

For we know,
That, whatever happens,
Our final resting place will be
Inches from here.

Our final moments,
Our last few living breaths,
Now we accept that we are just,
Inches from the end.

The end of our story,
Of what could have been,
We are on our last few,
Inches of page before...
Silence.

Ben Joseph Bowles (14)
Okehampton College, Okehampton

A SPELL TO CREATE LOVE

Essence of angel,
Unicorn blood,
A perfect diamond,
Red roses of love.

To make a fairy tale love,
Powerful and true.

Orange silk,
And golden locks of hair,
Green limes to add a zesty spark,
Fluffy clouds from the bright blue sky.

To make a fairy tale love,
Powerful and true.

Indigo irises,
Violet lavender,
A sprinkle of fairy dust,
And candy sweetness.

To make a fairy tale love,
Powerful and true.

The spell is nearly complete,
But first we must add,
A drop of sunlight,
And the rainbow.

To make a fairy tale love,
Powerful and true.

Florence Griffiths (12)
Okehampton College, Okehampton

THE SNOWMAN

He was a tank,
Driving through a battlefield of freezing cold bullets,
As the hail-fire lashed against him,
Gashing his snow created skin,
his face strained because against his cold skin,
The snow was shoved.

Suddenly, he was himself again,
Sitting in the darkness of the night,
Abandoned by his creators,
He was alone… once again,
As dawn approached,
He waited, listening, watching, on a lonely adventure.

As life awakened around him,
The trees started waving,
The birds started stirring,
The roof started weeping,
As the ice started thawing.

The grey sky seemed weightless,
A jagged blue stripe cut through the dark grey horizon,
He started to feel the hopelessness,
As his life started slipping away around him,
And all that was left was a carrot,
Abandoned on the glistening grass…

Harry Tucker (11)
Okehampton College, Okehampton

LITTLE ROBIN SINGING

Little robin singing
Little robin singing
Little robin singing the beginning song

Little robin singing
Little robin singing
Little robin singing all day long

English and German fighting
Only in one pair of eyes
Is this delighting

Then Christmas comes to stop the fight
This it does
With all its might

Both sides advancing together
This will be a first
And last forever

Match after match
Trade after trade
Lots of friends being made

Then the end of what was for evermore
First and last
Then again... war!

Charley Harcombe (12)
Okehampton College, Okehampton

FALLING IN LOVE

Petal of flower, thorn of rose
Magic dust powder, water from hose.
Glowing stone from the enchanted lake,
Add it in but give it a shake
Cotton candy from the fair,
And don't forget bubblegum from someone's hair.
Lots of sugar to make it sweet, so you'll fall in love with
the man you meet.
Stir and stir and mix it all up,
And you'll fall in love quicker than a pup.
A box of chocolates from Valentine's Day,
You know, the ones you bought because he didn't want to pay,
Try not to forget the stuffed bear too, that blue one that you named
Boo!
Stir and stir and mix it all up,
And you'll fall in love quicker than a pup.
That's the end of the potion, to make the man feel a
different emotion.
You'll fall in love don't you worry, don't be too long. Quick, hurry.

Chloe Marie Walker (12)
Okehampton College, Okehampton

WORLD WAR ONE

In Flanders fields where soldiers lie
poppies grow that make us cry,
as time goes by the crying stops
as work goes on from day to day,
our thoughts go back to days gone by
when we played in the fields
where soldiers now lie
we will always remember you,
with our poppies on our hearts.

Ella Caitlin Dannan (12)
Okehampton College, Okehampton

SISTERS

I would tell you,
But I could give you a clue.
I could leave you,
With nothing to do.
I could help you all the way,
Or I could torture you day by day.
I could show you a path to follow,
Or I could leave you with no tomorrow!

I would listen to your stories,
I would help you brush your hair,
But I'm really very busy, so I'll pretend I do not care.
I would sit and play your games,
But instead I'll just call you names.

I know I can be a meany, admit it is true,
But you're my little sister, I'll do anything for you!

Cara Dixon (11)
Okehampton College, Okehampton

STAR WARS 7

On an adventure throughout the galaxy,
An unlikely hero emerges from the depths of Jakku,
And a friend is here, wearing armour of villainy,
Trying to destroy the First Order anew.
The Resistance are built to destroy the Empire,
But in the mist is a hero arisen in the Force,
To help demolish the Empire in fire,
But first she must take on a course.
She was ready, and steady and learnt it well,
And before too long her power was strong,
Her time had come and the Order fell,
The Starkiller was destroyed before too long.
Then the challenge came to seek an old master,
He would help her in the Force and she'd learn it faster.

Liam Balman (12)
Okehampton College, Okehampton

MRS MOON

Is Mrs Moon made of cheese?
Does she have very knobbly knees?
Is she close,
Or far away?
Where does she go during the day?

How does she stay in the sky?
Does she have wings to help her fly?
Is she happy,
Or is she sad?
Is she very, very bad?

Does she have arms,
Or legs,
Or hair?
Does she share secrets with moon bear?
If only I knew Mrs Moon.

Corren White (12)
Okehampton College, Okehampton

MY HARBOUR OF A THOUSAND LIGHTS

Darkness creeps up the beach,
A silent wave.
Light bears a knife,
A silver shadow.

A single swipe,
And darkness falls,
Down the beach,
Past the harbour walls.

Mouseholes' lights,
A fearless army!

A thousand waves lap the shores of a thousand lights.

Ruth Frangleton (11)
Okehampton College, Okehampton

WAR

Death is bound to be his destination,
On the battlefield he will see his end,
Pain is the next stop at the dreaded station,
He can either choose to attack or defend,

Sorrow will slice through a man like a spear,
The thrill of the mission starts with a gun,
Before he departs, he'll cry one last tear,
Young boys are mistaken, war is no fun.

Screaming bombs fall from the large birds above,
Gunshots echo through the lonely valley,
Sights of sleeping men people used to love,
The death of men is kept as a tally.

The sounds of sharp screams people deeply fear,
The war is no fun, boys, I would stay clear.

Katie Chapman (12)
Okehampton College, Okehampton

MY FRIEND THE ENEMY

It was dead of night,
I woke with a fright,
Bombs were falling all around,
Reverberating through the ground.

Quick, to the Anderson shelter,
Helter-skelter!

Little did I know a pilot had bailed out,
This would change my life without a doubt.
His stricken plane had come down,
On the outskirts of our little town.

My friend, Kim, and I, we found Hans in Scarlet Wood
We wanted to help him, if only we could?

Joe Manners (11)
Okehampton College, Okehampton

PEACE AT LAST

After war, all is quiet,
This field has lost the sound of riot.
Each poppy is a sign of remembrance and war,
Every man has their mark, rich or poor.
Bobbing redheads are scenic but a gory sea of blood,
For poppies grow in the churned up mud.
I can't talk for my loss,
He took control, he was my boss.
The sky is blue, the grass is green,
No war planes are to be seen.
Here I lie, in this field,
All those young men's lives were sadly sealed.

Mari-Grace Baldwin (11)
Okehampton College, Okehampton

TEDDY BEAR

The nights grow dark
As my thoughts grow deep
I think of the stars and how they resemble your eyes perfectly
How they sparkle in the moonlight
I think of the moon and how it resembles your smile wonderfully
How it is big, white and wonderful
I think of the warm breeze, how it reminds me of the feeling I get
when you're around me...
So warming and welcoming
I look at you and I picture a teddy bear
And how you are a teddy bear...
So loving and gentle.

Shannon-Rose Maben (12)
Okehampton College, Okehampton

THE EASTER BUNNY

The Easter Bunny's in a flap.
He'll never get it done!
Every year, it's just the same.
He's such a hot, cross bun!

He taps upon the hen-house door.
Hoping that they've been busy.
The hens look at his hopeful face.
He's always in a tizzy!

They fill his basket to the brim,
With eggs of every size.
There's brown and white and speckled ones
And some could win a prize!

The busy bunny hops and skips,
All round and round the towns,
To make quite sure the children wake
With smiles and not frowns!

But what is this? There's one egg left.
He checks his list to see
If anyone has been left out
'Oh, yes!' he smiles. 'It's me!'

William Bennett (12)
Okehampton College, Okehampton

HER

Who is she? That fair maiden.
I wish I knew her name,
Floating, hovering like an angel,
Amidst the human frenzy; she came
From a foreign land, an alien world,
Wit her bronzed tan,
Her smooth-as-silk Latin speak
And a body that could only be found in the dreams of a young man.

So elegant, so sleek, so... mesmerising.
Not quite a hypnotic trance,
Unless, of course, the mysterious beauty,
On the spur of the moment, decides to dance.
Beautiful lady, smile so gentle,
Please stroll with me under the setting sun,
Why won't you kiss me?
Kissing is fun...

I still remember her vividly,
Five years on,
Those piercing green eyes still searching my soul,
Looking at me, the one she couldn't take a chance upon.
But, alas, it wasn't to be,
This fleeting meeting nothing but a fantasy,
Conjured in the mind of a desperate loner,
To fill the void of an emotional cavity.

Craig Latimer
Portora Royal School, Enniskillen

THE DROP

There are so many sports with a thrilling ride
And some with a beautiful view,
But the best of them all is for people who fall
With their arms spread wide in the blue.
They thrill to the sound, high above the ground,
To the pressure of air so clean.
But high in their wake, there's a parachute brake
And they're part of a beautiful scene.

When the parachutes open in a thundering
It is time to fly back to the ground,
Where the picking is done to prepare for the fun
And the talk of their thrills can be found.
In so short a time they are ready once more
And two engines roar, and they gaze out of the door
As it lifts from the ground once again.

There once was a time someone spotted the load
To the exit point, where to get out,
With technology's flare, it's soon found in the air
But the GPS leaves room for doubt.
But that is forgotten in the desire to fly
As the jumpers all crowd the door,
They're ready for flight and they get the green light
And so quickly their feet leave the floor.

Joshua Kennedy
Portora Royal School, Enniskillen

PEACEMAKERS

Watching over concrete pillars,
they stand. Still, emotionless.
Raising hands to salute
I pause.

The peacemakers now pointed.
The future sits and rules,
'All citizens must raise and obey
for good of country, family...'
I wait

While hurrying, scurrying,
burrowing into the recesses.
Any security now vanished;
the individual now shown but yet
never listened to.

I clench my fist
and show the signal.
Peacemakers now screaming,
firing, fighting.
My work now drained,
I fall and silence

Stops.

Tully Irvine
Portora Royal School, Enniskillen

SCHOOLS THESE DAYS

Schools these days are a disgrace
They never fail to take the smile off my face
Every time you think you've got a break
They give you more work to make your wrist ache
How much free time do they think we get?
They think we have all the time in the world, I bet
When am I meant to go and have fun
If I'm always sat at my desk on my bum
Doing work that won't benefit me
Because they want to take away my glee.

John Mortimer
Portora Royal School, Enniskillen

MY PAST

Started from the bottom now I'm here
didn't think the end was so near,
Look back to where I came from
when I was so young and dumb
Now I'm wild and free,
but don't have my family
Started a fight,
Used all my might.
But it all ended that night.

Alex Holder
Portora Royal School, Enniskillen

TOUGH LOVE

The tears and cries just flow out,
My love for her, I have no doubt.
The great moments and times we shared,
Our polar personalities could not be compared.
That one tranquil time at the beach,
She was never too far, I only had to reach.
The waves crashed and the water tickled our toes,
Our relationship back then, it had no woes.
Our feet sank into the deep, dark sand,
When I was in trouble she was always on hand.
The heat of the sun sizzled our backs,
Those times when I was near her, my body would relax.

But now, these days have trickled away,
All I wanted was for her to stay.

Jake Browne
Portora Royal School, Enniskillen

BELOW

The thing swam beneath our feet,
Down there, it stared at us like meat,
It's coming for us, the Human Fleet.
Still, and always coming, an athlete
Of death

By then we knew our time had come,
All our bodies were completely numb,
Our hearts in our mouths, beating like a drum.

No use trying to stay and fight.
No time to try and break its might.
No way would we make it through the night.
By this time we were now glistening white,
Waiting, always waiting for that horrendous sight.

Richard Henry Francis Falkiner Pendry (16)
Portora Royal School, Enniskillen

THE FUTURE

Our future on Earth, flying cars.
Holidays and day trips to the stars.
What will this planet soon be?
The wonders of technology we're yet to see.

New phones, flying cars and virtual reality.
With all of this technology will we need a holiday?
A safe haven with no gadgets to be seen,
Like a rehabilitation centre with addicts going clean.

Clear head, clean mind, no screen near,
A place without a phone sending messages of fear.
Surely all of this is bad for our health.
Here are the days when life is about wealth.

Ronan Cummins
Portora Royal School, Enniskillen

LIFE HAS CHANGED

Humans used to be just skin and bones
Now our hands are replaced with phones
Our robotic body, our metallic soul
Our human bodies that were stolen.
I feel no pain, I have no doubt
That life was better before the drought.
The land is dry
No birds would fly
The world is dying, day by day
No robot in this world has a say
Nothing will ever be the same
The entire world is in pain.

Dylan Johnston
Portora Royal School, Enniskillen

161

THE MESS

Broken bottles and smashed bits of glass,
Drink cans and wrappers lying in the grass.
Our oceans are being filled up with oil,
While harmful chemicals are destroying our soil.
Across the world, they are tearing down trees,
Who knows how big this mess will be.
The problem we face is the end of mankind,
So don't leave the next generation to tidy the mess we leave behind.

Aaron Elliott
Portora Royal School, Enniskillen

HOMAGE TO ROBERT FROST

(Inspired by 'The Road Not Taken' by Robert Frost)

Two roads diverged in a yellow wood
And faced with a choice, I stood
Amongst flowers of reds, greens and blues;
Pondering which way to choose.

One path is trimmed and trodden bare
The other is unkempt like tangled hair.
But deciding on which way to go
Was hard, so I pause for a moment or so.

Which is better, the second or first?
(One will be best, one will be worse)
Nothing to guide me, no sign nor post
So I'm taking a path that stands out the most.

What will be next on this journey strode?
Alas, another fork in the road.

Ruth Harrison (13)
Priestnall School, Stockport

FALLING APART

Cracks,
They spread across the surface like wildfire,
Ignited so easily, so quickly,
By the simplest of triggers, by harsh words,
Long, intricate lines which weave their own path,
Sometimes deep trenches or shallow, thin streams,
They decorate each monument differently.

Flooding,
One by one each crystalline drop descends,
The flood is accompanied by far more,
Falling soldiers glistening on the stone,
One, then two, then ten – they all fall slowly,
The thin cracks hastily join together,
An intricate pattern of grand carnage,
Each segment then falls – varying in speed,
Until no armour is left.

Cracks no longer decorate the surface,
It is plain and raw and almost flawless,
Vulnerable – and desolate – empty,
The walls have fallen down, they are left bare.
Halted, the flood is now a sudden draught,
Their strength is banished in this one moment,
As if nothing more than smoke in the wind,
Confidence gone as if a stolen breath,
Barriers do not protect their fortress,
Just one crack – they are naked, defeated,
Hollow.

Hannah Zoe Payne (17)
Reigate College, Reigate

BEING ME

Inside my mind, the beat goes on
Creating new sounds
But not for the masses
My world is pretty
And full of mysterious wonders.
Especially cats.
Friendliness prevails, rudeness confuses
A logophile at heart, vocabulary in my mind
distracted
By the things
I thought only I liked.
They clog the drain
'Sunshine and rainbows!'
Says my voice
'Everything is stressful.'
Says my mind
Yet nothing is stressful
Shared.
Family and friends
make me feel
Good again.

Claire Neeson
Rosshall Academy, Glasgow

BEING ME

It's true, I know,
Not everyone shares my interests.
From crows, to latex and alcohol paint,
I make myself gruesome, I can't help it.
It's true, I know,
That not everyone shares my interests.
Society, doesn't understand why
I am utterly infatuated with grief,
Why I have a thing with feathers.

I could try and make a character
After all, it's what I do best.
The rasp of grief, the thing with feathers.
My skin is white and translucent. I can't help it
Not everyone shares my interests.

Finally, here we sit and smile,
I can only watch.
What can I do about it?
Because not everyone shares my interests.

Shauney Patrick (14)
Rosshall Academy, Glasgow

VANISHING

Drop by drop
Falls from the tree leaves
I count the time
That reels to their trunk
And falls on the earth
With the leaves
That turned blonde
At its pass
While the sun
Still rises
One last
Breath
Dew
Before we hear
The trees' cry

Dreams that vanish
In fading stars
In the light of the lightning
Everything ends
The rain
The support
We're seeking
In a world that
Disappoints us
While the faith/hope
For a new start is
Eliminated.

Varvara (Vera) Tzoanou (16)
Royal Alexandra & Albert School, Reigate

THE FERAL KING

She is a King
Feline incisors crowd her wide-splitting mouth
Gums like deep dark tar
Her blood red eyes swell like Jupiter
Opulent and milky white to the dead sky
Gore crusts underneath her falcon-like claws
Dead leopards at her arms
She wrenches inwards, muscles and tendon rippling the black
membrane
Deformed wings peel wetly off her back, pallid and jaundiced
With the sick of disease
The surface like a hot, putrid sponge
Two useless rotting limbs
The defect of God
She rules and measures every breath
The cause of creation
The cause of carnage
She is a King
She is the King

Zanett Schiller (18)
Royal Alexandra & Albert School, Reigate

I WAS A SLAVE

I was a slave,
Born to work and make,
Cotton, wool and tobacco.

Once a free man was I,
Treated like an actual human was I.
Roamed, through the gardens with my family,
Till, I was captured and taken to sea.

All the things that made me, me
Stripped apart,
Nowhere to be seen.

Then I was taken to the West Indies,
Didn't like it at all,
So I begged on my knees.
Because I wasn't like Kunta Kinte,
Strong and bold.
Next thing I knew I was sold,
Sold to the white man,
To the white man I was sold.

I was a slave,
Born to work and make,
Cotton, wool and tobacco.

Precious Grace Ogunlowo
Sacred Heart Catholic School, London

CALMLY, I WALK

Calmly, I walk through a rose garden, one so beautiful
that no coincidence
could've led me to it,
My eyes are closed, fingers outstretched to touch the delicate petals
of the nature around me,
I embrace the cool wind which kisses my face and smile with content,

The dew-covered grass feels cool beneath my feet,
And, to me, the buzz of bees is therapeutic,
Slowly, I sit down, cross legged to take in the breathtaking
surroundings,

To make this memory last, I go to pick the brightest, biggest,
boldest rose,
However, my index finger and thumb meet a tiny but fierce thorn,
It is only a little cut against my vast and pale skin but the necessary
damage is done,

As humans, maybe we should aspire to be that rose,
Beautiful and admirable but tough for the right reasons,
Let's be more than just 'pretty'.

Elizabeth Mary Bratton (13)
Sir John Lawes School, Harpenden

SEVEN HEIGHTS OF MASTERPIECE – GENESIS

Heavens, he who speaks light will create mankind,
He who presents this galaxy of type,
A creativity of not a simple mind,
The heavens and God, little they knew the apple would be ripe.
The light is present, the darkness awaits,
Causing segregation between the rivals,
Soon there he shall present the new arrivals.

The skies a clouded blue, to be or not,
The fortress that smothers the sphere is painted in all sapphire,
The intricate way in this work cannot be created in sot,
The difference in place will never be razed with black fire.
Blue is the colour of the rhythm within,
Kindred air is tranquil,
Not a layer or a pinch lay with sin,
What silence may live will be lost at will.

Soil and land, fresh dirt, this scent demanded life,
Swarming with slid particles, new to this world, as is everything,
It was perfect, yet future held strife,
God thought good things, so committed like a special ring.
Heaven to soar and live in the sky,
Lands below gazed upon the sacred light,
Silence will be eternal rarity, not a whisper, not a sigh,
God had plans that will be at use, of course he might.

Time shall be at track,
Time shall be counted amongst fiery blazes,
The flaming stars will never lack,
God will create more to his warmth and praises,
Black smeared the heaven's sky,
Though this sky was galaxy, miles wide,
No illusion, no trickery or lie,
Silence swarmed, no evil had shed or cried.

Silence was no more,
Sweet soundings of those who'd fly,
To those in the deep blues, not winged to soar,
Colours idyllic to those under and in the sky.

Vivid with cheer and happiness,
Animals of kind,
They were happily untroubled, at least I guess,
This is not by creation of a simple mind.

Creatures creeping on the Earth,
Tips of their fingers to the edges of their feet,
This world's proven its very decent worth,
Creatures of beyond what's known had no time for us to meet.
Populated with nature,
Lived beside God's masterpiece art,
Well, so far before the him and the her,
God was glad to have known his work had a live beating heart.

Alas! The seventh complete, now for God's great rest,
Wearied and tired led to him,
His creative work, too great to be kept on blueprints in a chest,
God gazed upon to admire.
Yet something started to think,
Something in his God mind,
The missing link?
The thought of mankind...

Charley-Ann Weir
St Mark's West Essex Catholic School, Harlow

MY BROTHER

My brother is annoying, he screams and screams and screams.
He is only four months old but his voice is so bold!
My brother's name is Zachary and when it comes to bedtime it's like
he runs on Duracell batteries
But sometimes my brother is cute and mild, he can melt my heart
with just one smile!
My brother's skin is soft to touch and I love him so, so much.
And although my brother is always crying, he is mine.

Rebecca Elsmore
St Mark's West Essex Catholic School, Harlow

MY HEADPHONES

My headphones,
The realm where music is,
Where frequency and wavelength rule,
And my head is free so I can wander.

Lyrics wander around my mind,
As I ponder and begin to find,
A meaning that's from the soul,
And to touch others is its only goal.

Rhythm flows through my veins,
As the sound takes me away,
And soon enough a smile will linger for a day,
While with my headphones I decide to stay.

Tia Kelchure (13)
St Mark's West Essex Catholic School, Harlow

WET WEATHER

My heart is racing, my eyes are fixed,
The dashing waves cold as ice, dance in the whistling wind.
Lashing rain, malicious waves, the two a petrifying mix.
My heart is a statue, fear has penetrated like water into wood

Worrying waves way up high, like a skyscraper,
Malicious clouds gather and cry all over us.
The breeze whines like a child, water over the acre.
My heart is petrified, the storm is a murderer.

Joanne Faulkner (11)
The Bishop Wand CE School, Sunbury-On-Thames

A POEM FROM THE FUTURE

When I got off the bus today
I was surprised to see,
That someone wasn't on their phone
Now that really surprised me!
I don't have an iPhone 1000 myself
But apparently, it's great!
The iPhone 6 is really bad
And seriously out of date.
The Hunger Games have been and gone
And I'm happy to let you know,
That a horrid man died in the process
And that man was President Snow!
All the people who were popular
Back in 2016
Have changed their places in the world
And I write this with esteem:
Thank goodness for my local pub
Where Donald Trump has gone.
Not making rude comments, just pouring pints
What I wanted all along!
And Kanye West, what can be said
For this rather memorable rapper,
Who is now the American president
With his face on a chocolate note wrapper!
I watch over our vast world
Now that I'm a ghost,
So I see all the silly things
That people do the most!
However, there are ups and downs
As I see your face begin to fall,
That when you become a ghost
You can get stuck inside a wall!

Lucy Draper (12)
The Bishop Wand CE School, Sunbury-On-Thames

THE STORM

The rain danced along,
Down in the street,
The fear crept around,
Like a pet with nothing to eat.

The waves rammed the shore,
Shaking the earth,
The tears were streaming,
For once, not with mirth.

The floodwater was rising,
Swallowing the floor,
Like an unwelcome guest,
Opening the door.

The houses were dying,
All things of the past,
People were praying,
For what they thought would be their last.

Jenson Beer (12)
The Bishop Wand CE School, Sunbury-On-Thames

YOUR BEAUTIFUL LOVE

Your beautiful love is like a fresh breeze,
I could spend years loving you as you are,
I will never stop loving you, Louise.
Our love in this world will go very far.
Your eyes shine brighter than a summer's day,
Keep me close in your heart, we will never part,
Your voice is as soothing as the calm bay,
Your lips are sweeter than a strawberry tart.
We will never be apart; death won't win,
Like an aeroplane our love is soaring,
We are like peas in a pod – you're my twin,
You are magnificent and adoring.
I will pour out my love for you always,
Our life together will break down doorways.

Thomas Hawthorn (11)
The Bishop Wand CE School, Sunbury-On-Thames

SONNET: MY LOVE

Your beautiful love is like a fresh breeze,
I could spend years loving you as you are,
I will never stop loving you, Louise,
You are my gorgeous, golden, shining star,
Seeing your flowing hair is the sunshine,
Gives me fluttering butterfly feelings,
I wish you could be always forever mine,
My loving heart pumps up to the ceilings,
Your cherry red lips are perfect to kiss,
Sweet scent of blossom reminds me of you,
Loving you is too hard to not resist,
You are the kindest girl I ever knew,
So let's go together on the same track,
I love you so much: to the moon and back.

Cerys Powell (11)
The Bishop Wand CE School, Sunbury-On-Thames

175

REGRETFUL SORROW

Mistakes are made, justice to some
Mistakes are forgiven to those who come
And express their faults, their wasteful ways
In the irrational truth of the coming days
My poor sense of doubt, a poor depiction
Not to follow the dreams of fiction
Spared belief, though minds are torn
Love so lost, or the lost to mourn
A shattered visage, a tattered garment
A state of decay – this unveiled debarment
Loses my vision of people, I hoped -
Purging once things I had once coped
Mistakes were made, promises to set
Mistakes are left to a life of regret.

Blake Robinson (17)
The Duston School, Northampton

THE MILKY WAY

The Milky Way,
Full of mysterious milk,
Weird rocks float,
The aliens as strange
as a dog called Barry.

The falling stars move,
As fast as a javelin train,
The Milky Way people must
Explore what kind of milk
Is found up there...

Space, a lot of space,
In that Milky Way,
Lost astronauts say, 'Wait, mate,'
The moon is bigger than nine thousand, two hundred
and thirty seven Babybels all put together.

James Friend (12)
The Ebbsfleet Academy, Swanscombe

THE FIMBLE FOWL

The Fimble Fowl,
With wooden legs,
Would often fly
above our heads,

The Fimble Fowl,
With leaves for wings,
Soars through the sky,
And joy it brings!

The Fimble Fowl,
Would say, 'Hello!'
To all the creatures
Down below,

The Fimble Fowl,
With colourful nose,
Would light the sky up
Where it rose,

The Fimble Fowl,
Has found its home,
Atop a fluffy cloud...
We hear it laugh,
Though it's up high,
Because it is so loud.

Sofia Elghazili (12)
The Ebbsfleet Academy, Swanscombe

MIDNIGHT HOUR

Siblings of the night, dressed in cloaks of black,
wander streets of earth and crawl out in the night.
There is no use hiding, found his sack to play,
a trail of voices whisper, frightened in the depths.
On pads grow daggers sharpened on tracks of stone,
a bark at midnight sounds too close by.
Through time-paths seeking, carrying treasure,
speed through flap of home.
Out of breath they sit,
drop their treasure in the room of chairs.
Lick themselves clean, scrape wood of claw,
go up the moaning things and there stands morning bright.
With sleepy eyes and so to sleep,
as day comes in from night.

Victoria Rose Potts (11)
The Ebbsfleet Academy, Swanscombe

AN ODE TO WI-FI

Invisible air-waves throughout our home,
Creeping and seeping through our doors and walls,
Allowing us to access Google Chrome,
Contacting our family through Skype calls,
Chats to our friends with social media,
Face-to-face talking is really quite rare,
Find things out using Wikipedia,
Wifi, I hope you will always be there;
You have good points, bad points but mostly good,
I don't know how I could live without you,
You have been with me through my whole childhood,
If you do vanish, I think I could get through,
You are just three curves and a dot,
However, to me, you mean such a lot.

Rachael Lewis (12)
The Ebbsfleet Academy, Swanscombe

THE TOUR DE LIFE

Deceased were all my many friends,
And it was at this point when
My mind was cast to life without
Those that'd gone whilst I was out
Doing jobs and minding my errands,
I hereby dawned on my despairing.
The thought of life just cycling on,
Without me to change its song;
To think of people living through
Life without me there too.
Is for light to shine without its source
Or for order to be kept, minus the laws;
The pen to write with no ink
Or a brainless body that is able to think.
This thought had come to me that morning.
Was it a test or a dream or a warning?
As I grabbed my bedsheets and pulled away,
I planned to pack the coming day.

Dom Smith (15)
The Hurst Community College, Tadley

ROAR OF AN ENGINE

The roar of an engine gives me such a rush of adrenaline
Being behind the steering wheel makes me feel as strong as steel.
Flying down the motorway like a lion catching its prey
The V8 twin turbo is pure power
0-60 in 2.8 seconds
Racing round the track
The V8 rolling down the bank
The V8 is no more
It has so much damage it looks like it's been to war.

Kieran Gunner (14)
The Rowans PRU, Chatham

A PROUD MAN

He's a rather proud man
Rather proud of his appearance.

Crisp suit
Tie just right.

Ship-shape shined shoes.
Lapel aligned.

Hair slicked left
Right hand tucked in his pocket.

The slightest little grin
Almost trying to say
'I told you so.'

He's a very precocious man
A man who knows.

Ryan Bell (15)
The Rowans PRU, Chatham

FOOTBALL

My favourite football team is Real Madrid
The best team in the world
My favourite team to play for, my dream!
Ronaldo, Bale and Benzema scoring goals to win the league
From Pepe to Ramos, defending like a wall
Isco and Kroos wining the ball
Rodrigues to Benzema, they find Ronaldo to score
The Bernabeu expects the title will be ours.

Stefan Petik (13)
The Rowans PRU, Chatham

YELLOW

Yellow as the sun that gleams radiantly in the sky,
Dancing his way around Earth,
Flaunting his famous magic tricks,
Nature's portrayal of Houdini,
Giving a single continent his full attention, his alluring light
While shying away from the others, leaving them in the mystery of
midnight

Yellow as the silk petals set symmetrically around the
proud buttercup,
Stretching their fluorescent bodies above the green stalk
that holds them,
Eager to sunbathe in the heat.
Buttercup, the children's flower.
Infants giggle with a lustrous glow under their chins,
Inquisitively using the buttercup to test and ask each other:
'Do you like butter?'

Yellow as the wealthy honey, accumulated from determined bees,
Collecting pollen from a multi-cultural population of flowers,
Before bringing the honey back to their beehive,
A beehive that hangs as a piece of abstract art,
As trees stand boastfully, modelling these earthy, designer handbags,
Minuscule hexagons are interlaced by artistic bees,
And the beehive. Oh, the beehive. The beehive resembles
intricate tapestry,
As it assembles masses of amber honey

Yellow.

Yasmine Abbott (17)
The Sixth Form College Colchester, Colchester

PROGRESS

The future! It shines so bright,
As glass towers rise up to show their might,
It's power, it's progress and prowess
With no indication that we rose from less.

How we abandoned our morals and our sense of humanity,
How we sacrificed so much to fulfil our vanity,
How we left behind the needy, the destitute,
How they were denied the future's sweet fruit.

But what of science, of research and facts?
We sold our advancements to fat aristocrats.
We sold our very souls to companies with shiny devices,
We ignored the warnings and gave into our vices.

Progress, the steamroller of our age,
It laid the foundations, it set the stage -
To push the boundaries of what we thought we knew,
We didn't just walk and run, we flew

Forward into the unknown, straight into space,
We ate our own culture, our history and our faith -
Turned into creatures as we lost our personality,
Created our own end, the dusk of humanity.

Marcus Bron Hewitt (17)
The Sixth Form College Colchester, Colchester

OH GOD IS THAT THE TIME?

Oh God, is that the time?
Half past two in the morning,
I should have learned my lesson by now.
Not to get lost in the pages of books,
Even if Holmes's case isn't solved.
But I want to know if Alice was dreaming!

No. For God's sake, go to sleep!

Oh God, is that the time?
No, wait...
What if Frodo doesn't make it to Mordor?
Will Miss Bennet fall for Mr Darcy?
But what if Hogwarts falls?

It doesn't matter, go to sleep.

Oh God, is that the time?
I just need to find out if Katniss survives,
And if Percy catches the Lightning Thief.
But will Hazel have a happy ending?

Probably not, this is John Green we're talking about.

Oh God, is that the time?
Just a second, I need to know if Langdon figures out the password to the Cryptex,
Oh wait, what will happen to Scarlett O' Hara?
What about Pip and Estella?

No, just please go to sleep!

Oh God, is that the time?
Just one more line, I tell myself,
One more page.
But...
The truth is I am not putting that book down until I finish it.

Morgan Chetah (13)
TMBSS, Oswestry

YoungWriters

Est. 1991

YOUNG WRITERS INFORMATION

We hope you have enjoyed reading this book – and that you will continue to in the coming years.

If you're a young writer who enjoys reading and creative writing, or the parent of an enthusiastic poet or story writer, do visit our website www.youngwriters.co.uk. Here you will find free competitions, workshops and games, as well as recommended reads, a poetry glossary and our blog.

If you would like to order further copies of this book, or any of our other titles give us a call or visit **www.youngwriters.co.uk**.

Young Writers
Remus House
Coltsfoot Drive
Peterborough
PE2 9BF

(01733) 890066
info@youngwriters.co.uk